DetailsforLiving

DetailsforLiving

Stephen Crafti

images
Publishing

Published in Australia in 2007 by
The Images Publishing Group Pty Ltd
ABN 89 059 734 431
6 Bastow Place, Mulgrave, Victoria 3170, Australia
Tel: +61 3 9561 5544 Fax: +61 3 9561 4860
books@imagespublishing.com
www.imagespublishing.com

Copyright © The Images Publishing Group Pty Ltd 2007
The Images Publishing Group Reference Number: 748

National Library of Australia Cataloguing-in-Publication entry:

Crafti, Stephen.
Details for living.

Includes index.
ISBN 9781864702491 (hbk.).

1. Architecture – Details. 2. Architectural design.
3. Architecture – Designs and plans. I. Title.

721

Edited by Robyn Beaver

Designed by The Graphic Image Studio Pty Ltd, Mulgrave, Australia
www.tgis.com.au

Digital production by Splitting Image Colour Studio Pty Ltd, Australia
Printed by Paramount Printing Company Limited, Hong Kong/China

IMAGES has included on its website a page for special notices in
relation to this and our other publications.
Please visit www.imagespublishing.com.

Contents

Contents (continued)

Introduction

Architectural details can transform the simplest house into a memorable home. While the spaces in a home provide a blank canvas, the details create the light and shade, bringing depth to the design in the process.

This book focuses on five key categories of architectural details: staircases, window treatments, joinery, fireplaces and skylights. While all the projects, like most homes, feature various combinations of these features, I have endeavoured to highlight the specific detail that defines each home, and makes a major contribution towards elevating it beyond the scope of the ordinary.

While each detail has a functional component – a staircase provides access to different levels in a home; a skylight provides additional natural light; a window provides ventilation and light – it also has a strong aesthetic component that contributes to the creation of architecture. These details, unlike a standard window or door, can be interpreted in numerous ways. And although the basic ingredients must be present, there's enormous scope to create a detail that's fresh and innovative and with an impact that is greater than the sum of its parts.

Each design featured in this book can be appreciated on its own. But they are best seen in the context in which they appear. An unusual window treatment, covering an entire façade, may initially appear unwarranted, given the amount of light it deflects. However, when the house is wedged between several public car parks or likely to be overlooked by neighbours, this detail not only appears appropriate, but fundamental to living in the home.

A section of the book is devoted to skylights. With contemporary living reliant on a sufficient supply of natural light, the success or failure of a design can be tied to the use of skylights. Some of the skylights featured in this book are cleverly inserted above kitchens, living areas and bathrooms. And while some are immediately apparent, others are ingeniously concealed. As densities increase, particularly in inner city areas, obtaining natural light via large external windows isn't always possible. So bringing in light from above, via skylights, is an obvious solution to this problem.

Superb architect-designed joinery is featured in one of the larger sections of the book. Increasingly, owners are requesting custom-made joinery, not only for their kitchens, but also for wardrobes, dining room credenzas and living areas. Having joinery custom made not only reduces the need to acquire furniture, it allows for integration with the architecture. While some of the joinery that appears in this book is relatively inexpensive, other designs are quite elaborate. In one house for example, the joinery is lavish,

with cupboards finished in woven silk, while the interiors feature mirrors to reflect the contents. Other designs are more robust, appropriate for a kitchen environment. Cupboards may be in a simple, painted MDF, but the design of the unit is considerably more complex, with nooks and spaces considered to the utmost degree.

A house may include sumptuous details such as curtains and the latest in designer furniture, details that obviously enrich a space. And often, these elements are purchased as the result of suggestions made by the designers of these spaces. However, such details are not the focus of this book. The details presented here cannot be ordered from a store and delivered the next day or month. These details, often shown with accompanying drawings and plans, demonstrate the skills and expertise of talented architects and designers.

Stephen Crafti

STAIRCASES

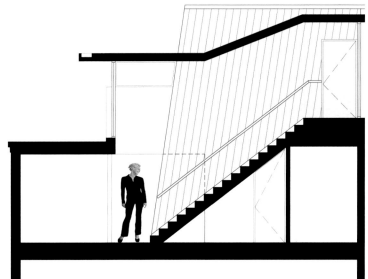

1930s apartment

Bent Architecture

The owners of this 1930s apartment desperately needed extra space. Their first-floor, 60-square-metre apartment had only one bedroom, a kitchen and bathroom and a small living area. "They weren't quite ready to move," says architect Paul Porjazoski.

To provide the extra space, a second level was added to the apartment by extending beyond the rooftop of the building. Using part of the existing hallway, the architects inserted a new staircase, which leads to a large living space and a small mixing studio (for music). The staircase features timber treads and plywood balustrades. Irregularly shaped openings are cut into the plywood.

"We wanted light to filter through the staircase and in the kitchen and living area," says Porjazoski, who also included two highlight windows at the top of the staircase to draw in the natural light.

The architects felt it was crucial to minimise the area of the staircase. "It's still a relatively small apartment. The only thing we had to remove was a built-in display unit from the original design," says Porjazoski, who saw the project as utilising basic 'infrastructure' to have dual functions. "The staircase is pragmatic (linking two levels) and also creates a lightwell," he adds.

PHOTOGRAPHY: SHANNON MCGRATH

Expressing materials 15

DP_Toscano Architects

Architect Joe Toscano used a limited palette of materials to renovate this inner-city Victorian terrace home. One of the main materials used was concrete, which appears on the floors in the new wing and is also expressed in the exposed concrete ceilings in the informal living areas. "Concrete and steel are the primary materials. So we wanted to use these in the staircase too," says Toscano.

An original staircase at the front of the house was retained. Featuring turned timber balustrades, this staircase leads to the main bedroom and parents' retreat. The second staircase, in the new wing, leads to the children's bedrooms and living area at the rear of the home; in contrast to the original Victorian staircase, it is minimal and pared back.

The new staircase features a gentle rise of concrete treads supported by steel rods that are connected to the concrete first floor. The rods, spaced 120 millimetres apart, double as the balustrade to the staircase. A balustrade on the first floor was eliminated by the inclusion of joinery. Painted a vibrant green, the MDF unit represents one of the few colours used in the interior. "We didn't want to introduce too many elements in the new wing. The design, like the staircase, is quite simple. We wanted to ensure the volumes and light are the main features in the renovation," Toscano adds.

16

Featherweight

Richard Kerr Architecture

Architect Richard Kerr wanted to design a lightweight staircase for this two-storey townhouse. Located on a relatively compact site (10 by 20 metres), it was important to create a sense of transparency through the house. Referred to by Kerr as 'Fallingwater' steps (after the house designed by Frank Lloyd Wright), the staircase is featherweight and aims to provide a rise that has an almost temporary appearance. "I wanted to dissolve any solid connection between levels," says Kerr.

The low-maintenance contemporary residence comprises an open-plan kitchen and living area on the ground floor, together with a powder room/bathroom. The staircase, located at the entrance, links with the two upstairs bedrooms, study and ensuite. While the 180-square-metre home appears relatively spacious, this is largely due to the open tread staircase.

The staircase is constructed from Tasmanian oak treads. On one side is a single Tasmanian oak balustrade (90 by 45 mm). Framing the treads on the other side are fine steel poles, spaced at 125 mm intervals. "The steel has been hung from the ceiling and joined to each tread," says Kerr. Steel angles, embedded in each tread, have been carefully positioned in the plaster wall to create a floating effect. Natural light enters through glass louvred windows and is dispersed through the kitchen and dining areas.

While light passes through the stairwell, sightlines are also created through the treads and towards an adjacent park. "The front window (adjacent to the door) is almost like a display window. You could see right through the stairs," says Kerr, who limed both the timber on the floor as well as the timber used for the staircase. "It just gives the whole space a slightly lighter feel".

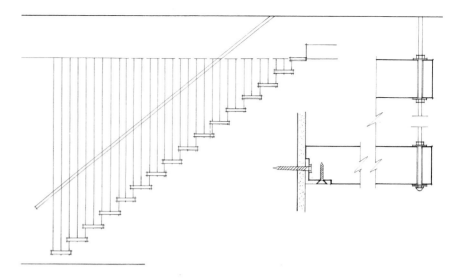

18

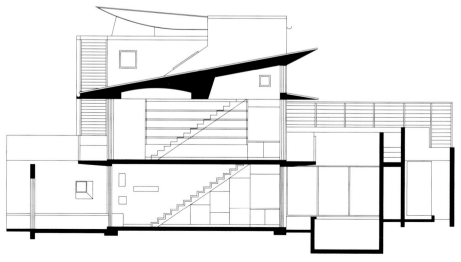

Japanese inspired

Keith Pike Associates

This staircase is located in a three-storey house that overlooks a waterfront reserve in Birchgrove, Sydney. The house has a strong Japanese aesthetic; a pond, for example, was designed adjacent to the front glass door and window. A bench, made of French limestone, was also built for the entry. "The idea is for people to take off their shoes, before moving into the house," says architect Keith Pike. "The area is similar to the Japanese 'genkan', the place to change from outdoor shoes into indoor slippers before stepping into the main entrance."

Irregular alcoves punctuate the wall at ground level. "They weren't designed for anything specific. I wanted to create some interest before ascending the staircase … it's more about creating shadow play," says Pike. In contrast, MDF cupboards below the stairs are functional and provide additional storage area.

The materials used for the staircase, which extends over the three levels of the house, change at each level. The first rise connects the two bedrooms, home office and garage to the dining, kitchen and living areas on the first floor. These treads are finished in French limestone and have been placed on a concrete riser. Limestone is used on both these treads and on the floors throughout the house. "We love the texture of limestone. In summer, it's cool under your feet and in winter it's heated by cable heating (constructed in the concrete floors)," says Pike.

The second rise of treads connects the living areas to the main bedroom and ensuite on the third level. Framed in steel that has been painted white, the staircase features toughened laminated glass treads. "We wanted to let as much light as possible into the ground floor," says Pike, referring to the skylight in the ceiling that filters light to the lower levels. This staircase is juxtaposed with a » glass wall with a rice paper insertion. "We wanted to keep all the materials as light as possible," he adds.

While light filters through the stairs during the day, at night, the glass treads glow with the assistance of artificial light. As Pike says, "The effect is quite magical. The staircase appears quite ethereal".

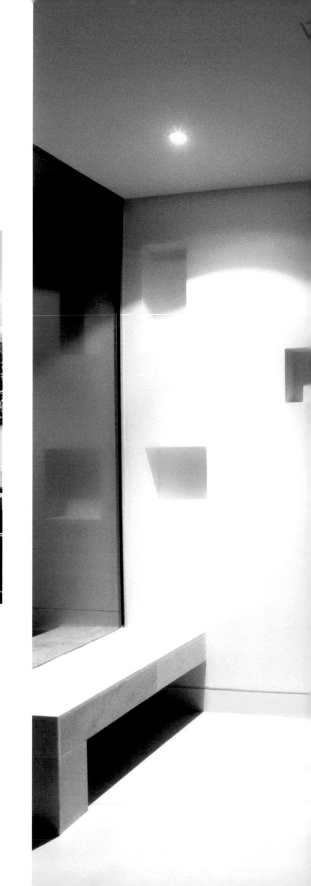

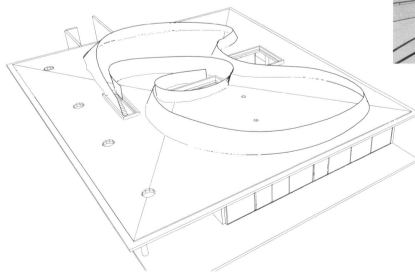

PHOTOGRAPHY: TREVOR MEIN, JOHN GOLLINGS

Like ribbon

Robert Simeoni Architects

Architect Robert Simeoni designed a large contemporary extension to a heritage-listed Victorian homestead. In contrast to the original timber home that features decorative fretwork, the new wing is sleek and minimal, framed by large floor-to-ceiling glass doors and windows.

While there is a strong juxtaposition of architectural styles, there is also a contrast between staircases in the old and new parts of the house. The homestead includes a romantic rooftop terrace with an ornate turret. "It's referred to as the widow's walk. Originally, the house was owned by a sea captain. When he went to sea, his wife would climb up to the turret, anticipating his return," says Simeoni.

The staircase in the new wing is external and accessed from the terrace. Ribbon-like in form, the sinuous staircase leads to a new rooftop terrace (above the concrete roof of the new wing). The staircase is made of reinforced concrete with an off-formed finish. The balustrades feature a curvaceous stainless steel handrail and expanding stainless mesh. While the mesh 'spills' out at ground level, on the concrete roof it has been arranged to enclose two distinct areas.

One area overlooks the heritage garden at the front of the property, while the other area overlooks the bay. "The shape of the balustrades was designed to reflect the dunes along the coast. But we also wanted to create something that was a contrast to the rectilinear lines of the new wing," says Simeoni.

The staircase has a sense of lightness, with the stainless steel mesh providing a contrast to heavier materials such as the concrete used in the new wing. "The design of the staircase is meant to be playful. But it's also designed to recede against the landscape," he adds.

PHOTOGRAPHY: TONY MILLER

Making a statement

SJB Interiors

This large penthouse apartment in Melbourne features two staircases. The more substantial of the two is a spiral staircase, which is located in the entrance, inside the front door. Cast in concrete and clad in limestone, it is framed by custom-made stainless steel mesh balustrades. "It looks like a ribbon that's been dropped," says interior designer Ljiljana Gazevic, a director of SJB Interiors.

While the spiral staircase has a certain lightness, it does appear to have been carved out of the limestone, with both the lower and upper levels surrounding the staircase also finished in limestone.

To illuminate the staircase at night, LED lights were inserted under the stainless steel handrail. "At night, it's quite beautiful. The mesh shimmers in the light," says Gazevic. The staircase was also framed with mirrored walls at the lower level. "You can see various parts

of the staircase reflected in the mirror. It heightens the sculptural form," she adds. The underside of the spiral staircase is as finely detailed. Finished in a wax Venetian stucco, there's a smoothness to the stair's undercroft.

Further into the apartment is a second staircase that leads to a gallery space where the owner's contemporary art collection is displayed. In contrast to the spiral staircase, this one is set between two walls. Embedded in one of these walls are Kreon lights, varying in height, to match the rise of the staircase. The American oak treads were stained an ebony colour to create a moodier approach.

"The two staircases are quite different," says Gazevic. "But they both work strongly with light, both from artificial lighting and with mirrored surfaces. We were keen to add a sense of drama, as well as creating fluid, well-connected spaces".

30

Multi-level journey
Multiplicity

This staircase extends across four levels of a 1920s warehouse that has been extensively renovated. What was once essentially a shell is now a fascinating home. "There's a considerable amount of height to cover. So we wanted to create the sense of a journey as you climb each staircase," says architect Tim O'Sullivan, who designed the multi-level home with his partner and Multiplicity co-director, Sioux Clark, an interior designer.

The stairs at ground level link the entry, bathroom, bedroom and garage to the home's open-plan kitchen, dining and living areas on the first level. A large coir mat greets visitors upon arrival. It has been embedded in the polished concrete floor at the foot of the stairs. From there is a gentle rise of treads finished in yellow tongue boarding stained with a black-brown pigment.

Once past the first corner, the second rise of stairs takes visitors by surprise. The staircase is placed under a four-storey light well

(existing void) and has been cleverly framed with the use of acrylic diffuser panels, originally intended to diffuse fluorescent lights. "We found these panels (1250 millimetres long by 300 millimetres wide) in dumpsters. We wanted to create a sense of transparency, both in how the light passes into the living spaces as well as with artificial light at night," says Clark, who strategically placed a couple of lights behind a few of the panels.

"Some people have compared the panels to a cityscape," says O'Sullivan, who used steel angle sections to form balustrades. "The panels also create a sense of privacy to the living areas," he adds.

A separate set of stairs leads from the living areas on the first floor to the bathroom, outdoor deck and main bedroom, the latter being on the highest level. To differentiate this staircase from the others, it was placed behind a translucent polycarbonate screen. "You can see people moving up and down the stairs from the living areas. »

But it's only their blurred silhouettes," says Clark. And like most great staircases, there's a surprise at the end of the journey. Outside the main bedroom is a steel grille on the floor, placed directly above the void. As Clark says, "it's quite a dramatic view of the void. And the city really comes alive from up here".

34

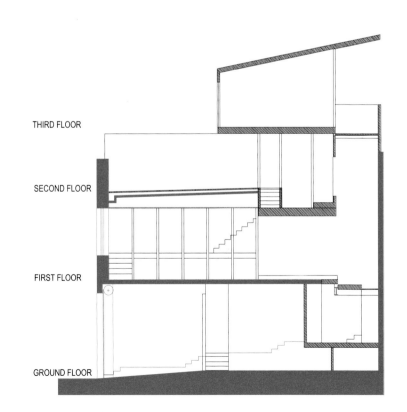

THIRD FLOOR

SECOND FLOOR

FIRST FLOOR

GROUND FLOOR

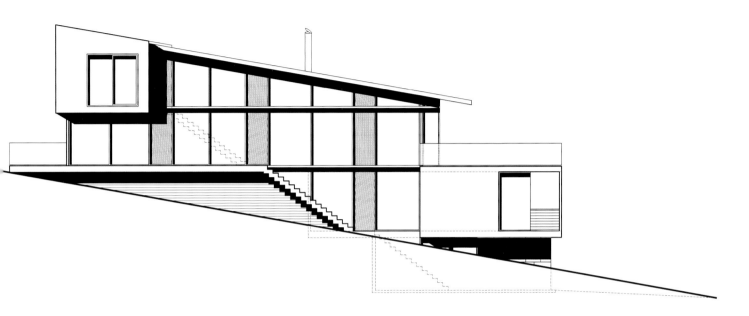

Over several levels

BBP Architects

This staircase is located in a beach house at Mount Martha, on Victoria's Mornington Peninsula. Linking several levels of the multi-storey house, the staircase follows a continuous line along the eastern wall as it spills down a steep site. "We wanted each level of the house to be segmented by a staircase. The idea was to create efficient spaces," says architect David Balestra-Pimpini, who designed the house with partner Serge Biguzas.

The staircase begins at the garage and forecourt and leads to two bedrooms, a bathroom and the laundry on the first floor. The staircase then follows the same path and connects these rooms to an open-plan kitchen, living and dining area on the second level. A mezzanine level, comprising two additional bedrooms and bathroom, forms the upper tier.

The staircase initially sits on a timber plinth at the entrance to the home. Framed by a rock garden that continues to a front forecourt, the staircase is evocative of modernist homes built in the 1950s. "It wasn't a conscious influence," says Balestra-Pimpini, "but I did want it to be fairly lightweight".

Made of steel (a steel box section supports the timber treads), the staircase is enclosed by a stainless steel handrail and steel wires used in the yachting industry. As one moves further up the house, the ceiling heights and walls enclosing the staircase change. At ground level for example, the staircase is bound with a solid wall. In the main living areas, the staircase is enclosed with a double-height frosted glass wall. The raked ceilings in the living area are more generous. "The spaces feel as though they're increasing the » further you walk up the stairs," says Biguzas, who enjoys watching the morning sunlight stream into the living areas through the frosted glass.

And to ensure the owners don't run out of breath as they proceed up the staircase, the architects provided generous landings at each level. As Balestra-Pimpini says, "the staircase isn't as daunting as it appears. Most of the time, the owners are in the living areas. So they usually only climb one set of stairs at any one time".

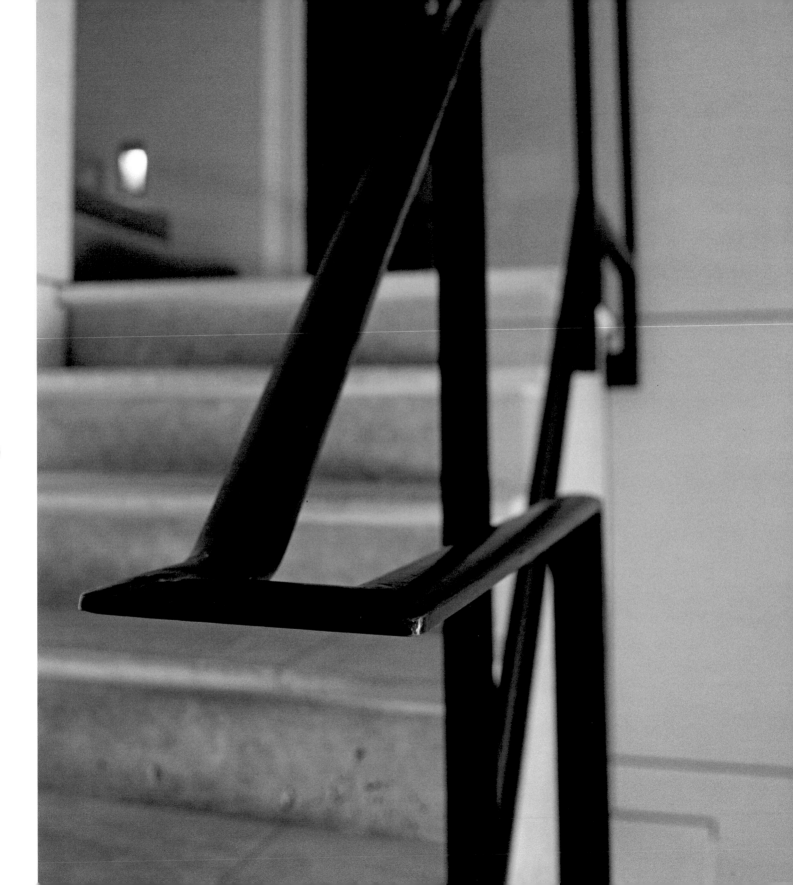

40

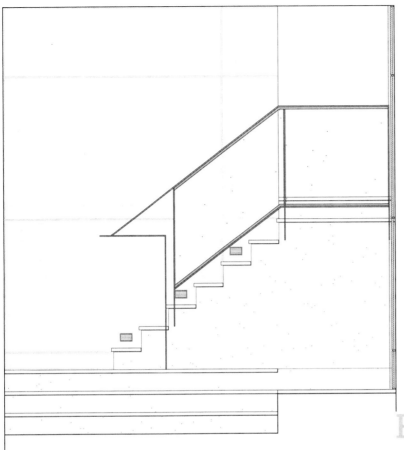

Refined detailing

b.e. Architecture

This staircase is located in the foyer of an apartment block in South Melbourne. The Victorian building was recently renovated and includes retail stores at ground level, with apartments above.

Because the entrance to the apartments is via a 4-metre-wide bluestone laneway, the owner requested a light-filled entrance. "Our client wanted the lobby to be fairly transparent, particularly with residents coming home late in the evening," says designer Broderick Ely.

Glass doors were inserted into the original tapestry brickwork and an entirely new foyer was designed. Polished plaster walls and ceilings were included in the design, as were new timber veneer walls and a limestone floor. Limestone, 30 millimetres thick, was also used on the treads of the staircase. "There's something quite special about limestone. It develops a wonderful patina," says Ely.

A simple graphic staircase was designed to complement the materials used in the foyer. Made of wrought iron, the lines of the staircase were inspired by the work of architect Pierre Chareau, who practised in the early part of the 20th century. "I've been a great admirer of his work. It's that level of detail that continually appears in his designs," says Ely, pointing out the detail in this staircase. "All the handrails are D-moulds and are comfortable beneath your hand. Notice the 'foot' detailing," he adds, referring to the junctions between the staircase and flooring.

Glass balustrades appear on one side of the staircase, giving it a sharp line. As Ely says, "the staircase wasn't a standard design. It's been carefully crafted. It's a one-off".

42

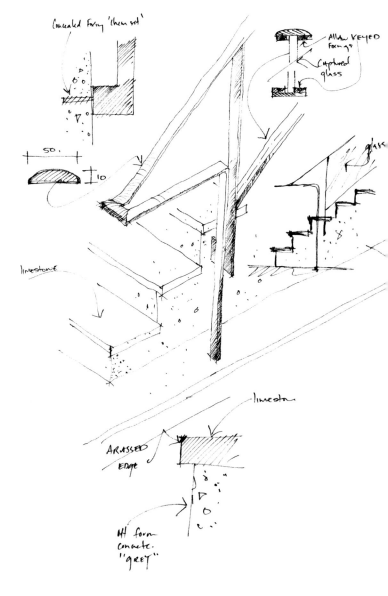

Reflecting the architecture

Fitzpatrick + Partners

The staircases in this new three-storey house strongly relate to the architecture. "The base of the house was treated like a solid mass, with the two levels above appearing more lightweight," says designer James Fitzpatrick.

A timber staircase leads from the kitchen and living areas and acts as the main spine linking the four bedrooms and bathrooms. The staircase also acts as a shield between the casual and more formal living areas in the house. "The owners have young children. They wanted separation, particularly when guests come over," says Fitzpatrick, referring to the plaster wall that separates the two areas. A toughened glass wall on the other side of the staircase provides a more transparent aspect.

The plaster wall contains large steel beams that support the individual steel plates used to support the timber treads of the staircase. Each steel plate has been fully covered in tallow wood, 20 millimetres thick on all sides (lower as well as upper). "The treads were treated like a glove. The timber slides over each tread," Fitzpatrick explains.

The staircase to the basement, which includes the garage, cellar, gym and plant room, is aligned with the staircase to the bedrooms on the top floor. However, rather than appearing to 'float', this staircase is considerably more weighty, like the external plinth for the house. "This staircase is like a hole in the ground floor. It feels as though you're moving into a cave," says Fitzpatrick. The treads and the walls leading into the basement are clad with studded rubber flooring.

Stop for a 'chat'

Phorm Architecture + Design

Architect Paul Hotston of Phorm Architecture + Design describes this Queensland house as quite eclectic. Several materials appear in the design, including steel, rammed earth, glass and polycarbonate sheeting. "The materials are fairly light, apart from the rammed earth, which acts as the spine of the house," says Hotston, who designed this house over three levels.

The staircase appears at the entrance to the home and links the entry, guest wing, rumpus room and pool courtyard to the kitchen, dining and living areas on the first floor. The lobby, which contains the staircase, features high ceilings and is framed on three sides by a polycarbonate wall with expressed blackbutt timber battens. "The staircase is really a bridging point between the living room on one side (first floor) and the kitchen on the other," says Hotston.

The staircase appears as lightweight as the polycarbonate walls. Featuring a steel handrail and stainless steel wires, the staircase has blackbutt treads that are supported by concealed metal cleats. The architects placed a podium-like timber base at the foot of the stairs (1 metre wide by 3 metres long). Juxtaposed with the polished concrete flooring, the timber staircase appears quite contained.

One wall of the staircase features a cantilevered timber 'chat chair'. Also made from timber, the chair is located opposite the kitchen bench on the first floor. "The chair feels as though it's part of the staircase. You can easily chat to someone in the kitchen or someone who has just arrived and is walking up the stairs," says Hotston.

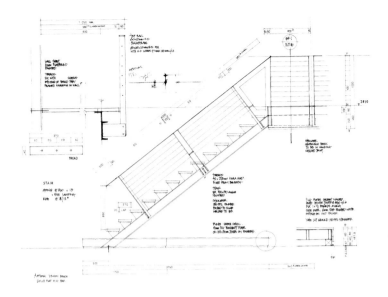

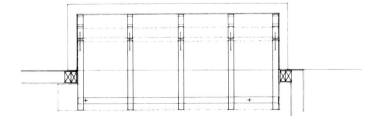

52

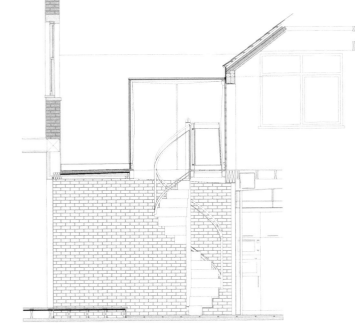

Two in one

Derek Wylie Architecture

This townhouse was renovated by architect Derek Wylie. Located in central London, the deep and narrow site offered limited views and little natural light. "The clients are a young family. They needed a design that felt robust as well as spacious," says Wylie.

Two staircases were positioned at each end of the elongated plan to improve circulation. Each staircase was strategically placed to suggest the function of each room, without the necessity for physical walls or partitions. "Both staircases were conceived as sculptural elements, which reveal their different configuration, support and construction," explains Wylie, who incorporated solid oak steps and fine mild steel structures in the staircases.

A spiral stair at the entrance to the home provides access to a mezzanine study space and the main bedroom. This staircase is fabricated from water-jet-cut plate steel, which is flush-welded to

provide the sharp, paper-fold edge undercarriage for the solid oak steps. The undercarriage is flush-welded to the circular support column to appear as a single form.

The main stair at the rear of the space uses a cantilevered, stepped metal edge plate, supported by a full-height mast that tapers towards its fixing positions at ground and truss level. The mast was constructed using a 90-millimetre circular support column, encased within an outer metal casing.

Guarding to both stairs is provided by steel weave mesh (normally used for stone grading), which naturally adjusts to the pitch, angle and curve of each stair. The mesh panels were edge clamped and bolted to the thin metal balustrades, which were flush bolted to plates welded to the edge of each stair.

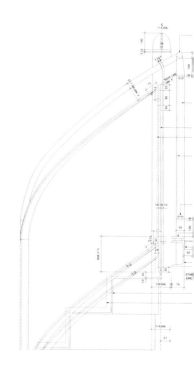

56

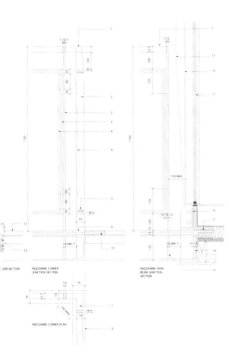

57

WINDOW TREATMENTS

PHOTOGRAPHY: KENNEDY NOLAN

Bar coded

Kennedy Nolan Architects

61

This Arts & Crafts home, built in the early 20th century, was once a rooming house. "It had been completely altered over the years. There were significant renovations in the 1980s and the following decade," says architect Patrick Kennedy. The entire house needed to be remodelled, some of the parts had to be restored and other parts removed.

A new kitchen and living areas were added on the ground floor as well as a new bedroom suite for the parents on the first floor. Two balconies were added to the parents' suite, which also includes an ensuite and dressing area. To ensure the neighbour's privacy, as well as protecting views into the main bedroom, the architects designed a 2.5-metre-high screen to cover the glass windows.

This screen, set well away from the glass windows, frames three façades (enveloping the home on two sides). The timber battens, which face the rear garden, are made of western red cedar and are supported on a steel frame. In contrast to the hue of the timber, the reverse side of the battens have been painted in 15 different shades of high-gloss enamel paint: turquoise, pinks, yellows, oranges and purple are just some of the colours used. "They're reminiscent of the inside of book jackets," says Kennedy, who varied both the width of the battens and the spaces between each one. "We wanted to create texture as well as a sense of depth," he adds.

Porthole-style windows were also inserted into the screen to provide a connection to the leafy garden. And although the screen wasn't strictly devised to minimise sunlight, it does form a 'fringe' over the living room on the ground floor. This screen also reflects some of the interests of the owners, who are keen on art and music. "It's quite a sculptural treatment. But the screen also activates the home's interior spaces".

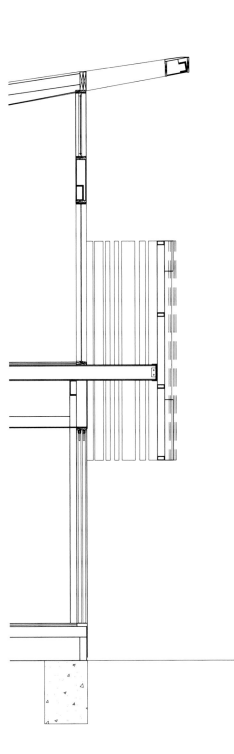

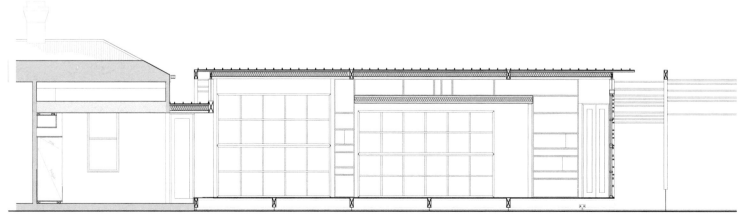

PHOTOGRAPHY: PETER BENNETTS

Building a dialogue

Andrew Maynard Architects

This double-fronted period home had several additions over the years. While the original Victorian rooms remained, a complete new wing had been added, and the kitchen and bathrooms had been refurbished. Rather than add a glass box to the rear of the home, architect Andrew Maynard was keen to turn the new wing inside out. "Sometimes the framework for a house is more interesting than the cladding. We wanted to create a dialogue between the original house and the new wing," says Maynard.

The new wing includes a main bedroom and ensuite bathroom. Oriented towards a courtyard to maximise the light, it is clad in cedar battens attached to garage doors/windows. Operated by concrete weights, the doors can be fully opened to the garden. "We wanted to blur the division between the interior and exterior spaces," says Maynard. Timber battens are also attached to the grey ironbark portal frames to form a second layer to the large expanse of glass. A 300-millimetre gap (small canopy) between the garage doors and the fixed timber battens provides some protection during inclement weather. "Even when it's raining, the owners can open up the doors completely," he adds.

The bathroom adjacent to the main bedroom is more exposed. As the house is on a deep site, overlooking the neighbours wasn't an issue. Nevertheless, to filter some of the morning light, Maynard also added timber battens to the tilt-up garage door in the bathroom. Where privacy is required, such as in the shower, textured and rippled glass was used. The battens were used to remove the hard edges from the extension, as well as diffuse the light.

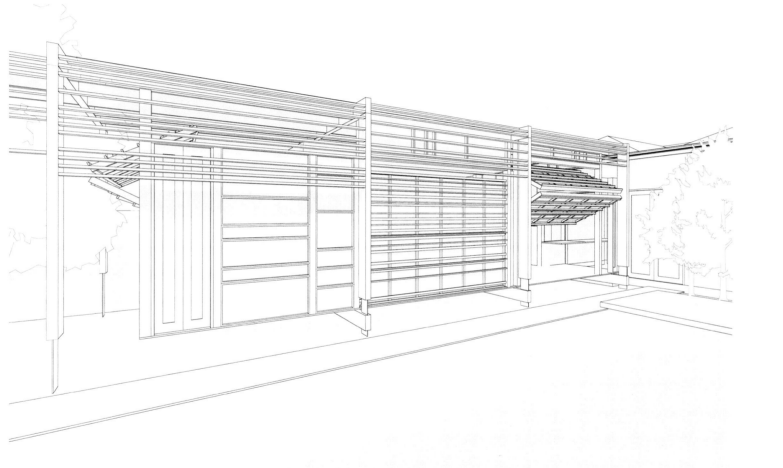

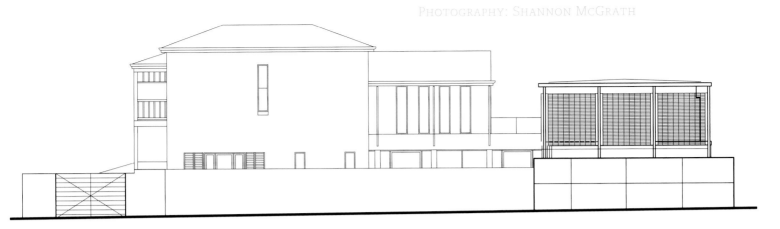

PHOTOGRAPHY: SHANNON McGRATH

Coming and going

DP_Toscano Architects

This semi-detached Victorian terrace is surrounded with cars. Located near a busy shopping centre, the house is adjacent to a large public car park. A relatively wide laneway (approximately 4.4 metres wide) separates the house from the car park; the laneway leads to a secondary car park to the rear of the property. With so many cars coming and going, the issue of privacy was crucial in designing the contemporary addition. "We wanted to reduce the visual intrusion of so many cars. And we also wanted to ensure sufficient light entered the home," says architect Joe Toscano.

A two-storey glazed box was added to the rear of the home, separated by a link or breezeway. Featuring floor-to-ceiling glass windows and doors, the new wing comprises an informal living area on the ground floor and the children's bedrooms and bathroom on the first floor. To ensure privacy, Toscano included an aluminium mesh screen on two sides of the house. Approximately 2.7 metres high, the robust screen acts as a balustrade while allowing light to pass through.

"The mesh is normally used for industrial platforms or walkways. It's all prefabricated. You look obliquely through the screen. The cars are just a blur to those inside," says Toscano, who used steel posts to support the mesh. "We could have reduced the amount of glazing in the new wing. However, our client wanted light-filled spaces," he adds.

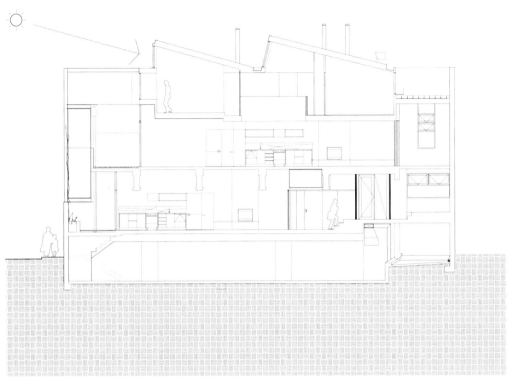

Constructing a view

Neometro Architects

These apartments were built at the same time as another set of apartments directly opposite. The view of the city slowly disappeared, replaced by red-brick walls and a series of walkways. "We knew the views of the city would diminish," says architect Karen Alcock, a director of Neometro Architects.

To ensure a 'respectable view', the original building was cut back by a couple of metres to allow for a garden aspect. "This building was originally a potato factory. The only outdoor space was the loading bay," says Alcock. Steel portal frames were added to the front façade, along with stainless steel wire that's been arranged in a diamond pattern. "We wanted to create a leafy outlook," says Alcock, who used the trellis-like screen to grow Virginia creeper. In only a few months, the creeper has spread to the second level of the

apartments. "It's a terrific vine. It turns from red through to yellow, depending on the season. The leaves always return in summer when they're needed most," explains Alcock.

The apartments on the ground floor feature concrete fences and planter boxes, which are raised slightly above the pavement level. The upper level includes operable awnings over the windows. "These apartments still have a view of the city. The awnings allow the residents to control the amount of light," says Alcock.

Fibreglass walls enclose the front staircase leading to the apartments; the light from within the stairwell creates a lantern effect at night. According to Alcock, "You're not conscious of being overlooked, whether you're climbing the stairs or sitting out on the balcony."

Inspired by Morocco

Stephen Jolson Architect Pty Ltd

Architect Stephen Jolson's design for a bedroom screen for this home was inspired by a trip to Morocco. A keen photographer, Jolson returned with images of a star pattern used in one of the Moroccan buildings. "I scanned the image when I came back. It took us five days to work out the geometry and how it could be used in the screen," says Jolson.

The finished design, which appears in a rusted steel screen, envelops an entire bedroom façade. "We wanted to create privacy as well as allowing the light to pass through," says Jolson, who wanted to screen the bedroom from the open-plan living areas on the other side of the courtyard.

The 6- by 3-metre screen was inserted into a heavy steel frame attached to the walls and roof of the main bedroom pavilion

(including a dressing area and ensuite). On the other side of the main bedroom is an angled glazed wall that has been designed as a natural 'water wall' to filter the morning light. Every time it rains, water cascades down the window.

While the laser-cut screen appears to have rusted over several years, the ageing process was accelerated by Jolson, who spent three days squeezing lemons over the steel. "The screen acts as a veil to the living areas. But it also creates its own unique light, with unusual patterns forming on the floors and walls," he adds. In the courtyard, Jolson planted a robina. Its colours, which change from green to gold, provide a contrast to the steel. "There's a wonderful contrast between the two textures, one natural, the other man-made," he adds.

A new layer

Six Degrees Architects

Six Degrees Architects regularly incorporates elements of the past into a new design. For this terrace house renovation in Richmond, Melbourne, it retained a Victorian façade with its ornate mouldings, as well as a 1970s bronze aluminium shop front that had been added to the ground floor of the two-storey building. While the two periods were integrated in the renovation of the building, an additional and more contemporary layer was added to the front façade.

A screen made of blue glass panels was attached to the façade. The 600-millimetre by 1.2-metre glass panels are dissected by glass louvres also made of blue glass with the same dimple pattern. "The glass isn't new. It was salvaged from the GMH plant in Dandenong. It was originally used to diffuse harsh sunlight in most factory situations. We used it to mitigate the west sun on the façade," says architect Simon O'Brien.

The 6-millimetre-thick glass allows both the Victorian detail and 1970s shop front to be clearly read from the street. The original Victorian windows on the first floor remain operable, with the louvred glass screen protecting the house from the harsh summer light as well as allowing a continuous flow of air. As the architects didn't want the hot air to be sandwiched between the glass and the building, steel angles were used to set the glass away from the building. As O'Brien says, "it makes sense to reuse materials. It's quite rewarding to rework materials to create something entirely new".

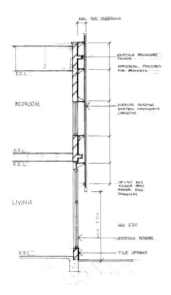

MAX. 300 OVERHANG

F.C.L.

BEDROOM

F.C.L.
F.C.L.

LIVING

F.F.L.

EXISTING BRICKWORK FACADE

HORIZONTAL POSITIONS FOR BRACKETS

VISTALOK GLAZING SYSTEM CONTINUOUS LENGTHS

100 x 50 RHS SINGLE SPAN REFER. ENG. DRAWINGS

EXISTING WINDOW

TILE UPSTAND

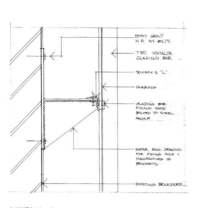

EPOXY GROUT M.R. MS BOLTS

T.80 VISTALOK GLAZING BAR

50 x 50 x 5 'L'

GLAZING

GLAZING BAR FIXING SHOE BOLTED TO STEEL ANGLE

REFER. ENG. DRAWINGS FOR FIXING SIZE + MANUFACTURE OF BRACKETS

EXISTING BRICKWORK

DETAIL 1
SCALE 1:5

80

EXISTING CONDITIONS

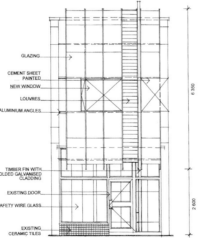

GLAZING

CEMENT SHEET PAINTED

NEW WINDOW

LOUVRES

ALUMINIUM ANGLES

TIMBER FIN WITH FOLDED GALVANISED CLADDING

EXISTING DOOR

SAFETY WIRE GLASS

EXISTING CERAMIC TILES

6.350

2.600

PROPOSED ELEVATION

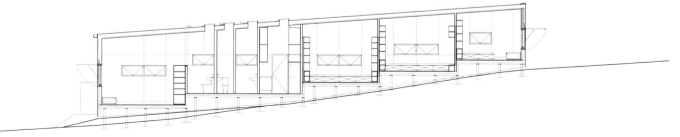

Opened and closed

Kerstin Thompson Architects

This beach house can be completely opened up upon arrival, or closed down, like a sealed suitcase, on departure. Clad in compressed cement sheet panels, it is evocative of many earlier beach houses built along the coast.

The house takes the form of two wings: one for the children and guests, the other containing the main kitchen and living area, together with the parents' bedroom, ensuite and study. A 'breezeway' connecting the two wings functions as the entry to the home, as well as the children's play area.

Architect Kerstin Thompson has treated the windows and doors in this house quite differently, depending on their use and orientation. The children's windows, made of the same compressed cement sheeting used on the exterior, are referred to as 'flaps' and are

simply pushed out, like the windows found in a caravan. As the children's bedrooms, along with the guest bedroom, receive strong afternoon sun, this treatment makes them appear to be relatively impervious. In contrast, the large glass sliding doors/windows on the opposite side of these bedrooms enjoy the softer morning light and have a double skin: one side glazed, the other with external perforated cement sheet sliding screens.

The main living areas are treated in a similar manner. One side of the living area is 'shut down', offering adjustable slot windows made of cement sheeting, while the other features perforated screens, identical to those used in the children's wing. The perforated screens are also a feature of the breezeway. On warmer days, the screens framing this space can be fully opened, while on cooler days, they are closed, while still admitting dappled light into the space. »

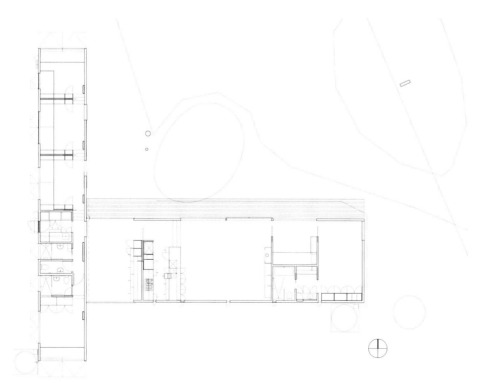

As mosquitos and flies are prevalent in this area, the architects included flywire screens behind the windows. But whether the windows and doors are left open or closed, there's a wonderful silhouette of tea trees against the cement. As Thompson says, "The house is really a canvas for these trees. And it's not a static picture. It continually changes with the light".

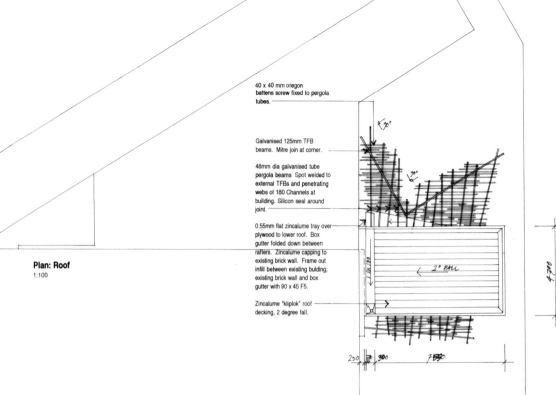

40 x 40 mm oregon battens screw fixed to pergola tubes.

Galvanised 125mm TFB beams. Mitre join at corner.

48mm dia galvanised tube pergola beams Spot welded to external TFBs and penetrating webs of 180 Channels at building. Silicon seal around joint.

0.55mm flat zincalume tray over plywood to lower roof. Box gutter folded down between rafters. Zincalume capping to existing brick wall. Frame out infill between existing bulding, existing brick wall and box gutter with 90 x 45 F5.

Zincalume "kliplok" roof decking, 2 degree fall.

Plan: Roof
1:100

2° FALL

Outside-in

Architect Janet McGaw

87

Architect Janet McGaw describes an extension to an inner-city warehouse as an 'outside-in room'. Framed by large pivot doors, the extension appears more like a breezeway between two outdoor garden spaces.

Originally designed as a bakery (circa 1916), the brick warehouse was later used as a workshop for signwriters. Sliding aluminium windows had been added to the building in the 1970s. There was also a steel roller door at either end of the building, allowing cars to drive through. In the conversion of the warehouse into a home, McGaw added a new kitchen and dining area to the rear and a garage with a deck over to the front. The interior of the original warehouse shell was completely remodelled. And in the transformation, she was keen to link the new extension to the garden.

The new wing, which is irregular in shape, slices the garden into two. To create the outside-in room, McGaw designed large timber-framed pivot doors. One of the doors is 3.2 metres wide, while the other is 2.4 metres wide. A salvaged steel-framed window is fitted within the oregon frame of each door. To create protection from the sun, two external sliding screens were included in the design. Made of plywood-faced solid core doors, these screens slide along a track and can be positioned depending on the elevation of the sun.

To further increase sun protection, McGaw designed external awnings above the pivot doors. Made of steel pipes, which continue through below the ceiling of the dining area, and covered with oregon battens, the awnings were inspired by the child's game 'Pick up Sticks'. "The sticks were dropped into place and screw-fixed where they landed," says McGraw. "When the doors are open, you feel as though you're sitting in the garden."

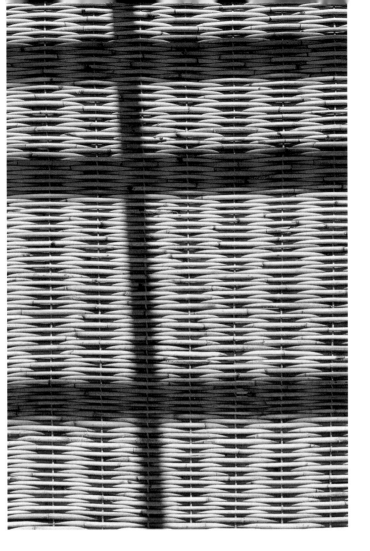

PHOTOGRAPHY: DEREK SWALWELL

Rattan screens

Architect Richard Swansson

This large Victorian home is surrounded by generous landscaped gardens. However, a previous 1970s addition to the stately home turned its back on the garden. "The focus of the room was a fireplace, set in a blank wall. There was no connection to the garden," says architect Richard Swansson.

The 1970s addition was completed removed. In its place is a two-storey pavilion-like structure, with floor-to-ceiling windows and doors on both levels. "One of the main issues was screening the harsh afternoon light. We wanted to open up the garden views without being overwhelmed by the heat, particularly during the warmer months," says Swansson.

In the ground-level living area, floor-to-ceiling glass doors were inserted into what was once a blank plaster wall. To diffuse the light, Swansson designed a screen. Made of rattan, the four-panelled screen is set behind the glass doors, like a retractable curtain.

However, unlike a curtain, these panels can be drawn back into cavity walls. A new external awning was also added. The original cast iron columns were incorporated, with the addition of new steel beams.

The same rattan screens appear on one of the windows in the main bedroom upstairs. These panels are placed on the outside of the windows to prevent the sun's rays from contacting the glass and thereby heating up the room. There is also an external steel balustrade across these steel-framed windows. "We wanted to create a softer edge to the design. We also wanted the light as well as the garden view to enter the home," says Swansson, who has always admired the use of rattan. "It's used a lot in tropical climates," he adds. And although the heat can take its toll on the rattan, he does suggest occasional oiling to maintain the colour. "Otherwise, it will turn a silvery grey. And that's quite attractive in this environment".

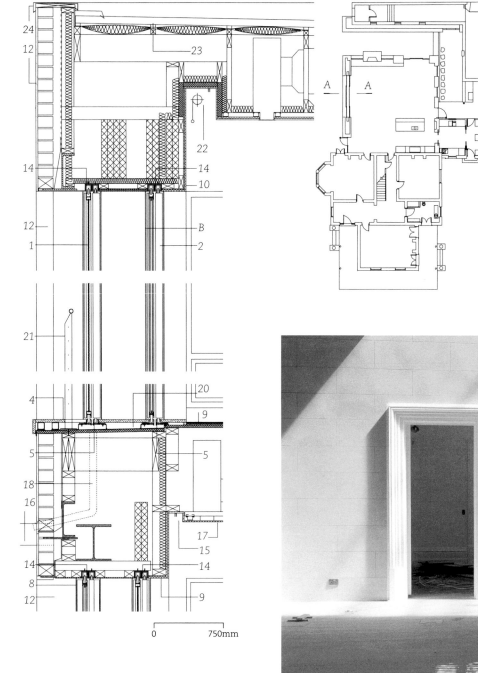

1   5 mm woven rattan on 2 mm stainless
    steel wire
    stainless steel threaded eyelets
    galvanised steel door frames
2   24 mm 6/12/6 double glazed unit
    low-E glass internally
    galvanised steel window frame
3   recycled 200 x 18 mm tongue and groove
    blackbutt timber floorboards
    70 x 45 mm timber joists
    100 x 45 mm bearers
    waterproof membrane
4   20 mm sawn Geelong bluestone
5   drained aluminium guide track
6   20 mm sawn Geelong bluestone
    random ashlar
7   10 mm cork strip in expansion gap
8   weather seal
9   2 layers of 10 mm plasterboard
    R2.0 bulk insulation
10 Graded concrete screed
    waterproof membrane
11 100 mm motorised aluminium blind
12 sand cement render

90

13 reinforced concrete slab
14 top hung sliding door track
15 100 x 50 mm shadowline curtain track
16 steel pergola
    150 x 50 mm galvanised rhs
    50 x 50 mm galvanised shs
17 10 mm plasterboard suspended ceiling
18 door cavity drainage pipe
19 carpet
    platform flooring
20 stainless steel sub sill
21 2 mm diameter stainless steel wire
    balustrade tensioned on swage screws
    32 mm diameter polished stainless steel
    handrail
    50 x 10 mm intermediate rail
22 32 mm mdf 220 x 220 mm pelmet
    block out blind
    curtain track
23 Colorbond secret fixed metal deck roofing
    20 mm foam spacers
    R2.0 bulk insulation below roof deck
    R2.0 bulk insulation above ceiling
24 Colorbond capping

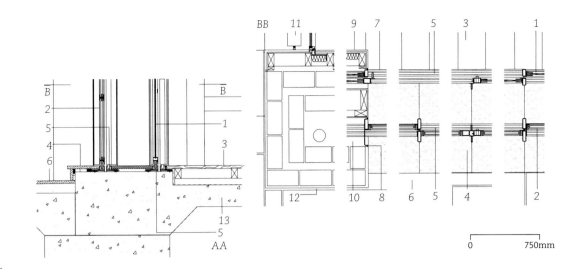

PHOTOGRAPHY: DAVID MARKS

Scaffolding

Architect Suzanne Dance

Architect Suzanne Dance has transformed this single-fronted timber cottage into a contemporary home. The original three rooms of the house were retained, while the lean-tos were demolished. "The house was fairly run down. There was no relationship to the garden," says Dance, who added a new kitchen and family room.

While the original rooms of the house, built at the turn of the 19th century, are timber, the new wing is made of steel. Dance followed the line of the pitched roof and created a new gable, also clad in steel. One of the most striking aspects of the addition is a steel pergola over a timber deck, leading to the rear garden. Almost identical in form to the scaffolding used by builders, the pergola is made of steel poles. While these poles are fixed with clamps, like those used by builders, the clamps in this instance have been welded together to form a permanent arrangement.

The pergola is temporarily covered with shade cloth, which will be removed when the deciduous vines can provide enough shade for the family room. One of the driving forces behind this window treatment was a mature spotted gum tree in the rear corner of the back garden. "I didn't want to use timber or a material that would compete with the beautiful colouration of the trunk," says Dance, referring to its wonderful marbleised colours, which range from greens to greys. The pergola stands apart from these colours and textures.

The steel used for the pergola ties in with the steel used for the windows and doors of the rear façade. As Dance says, "It's an industrial aesthetic. It may seem a little harsh in its present form, but it will be covered in a few months, at least during the warmer weather".

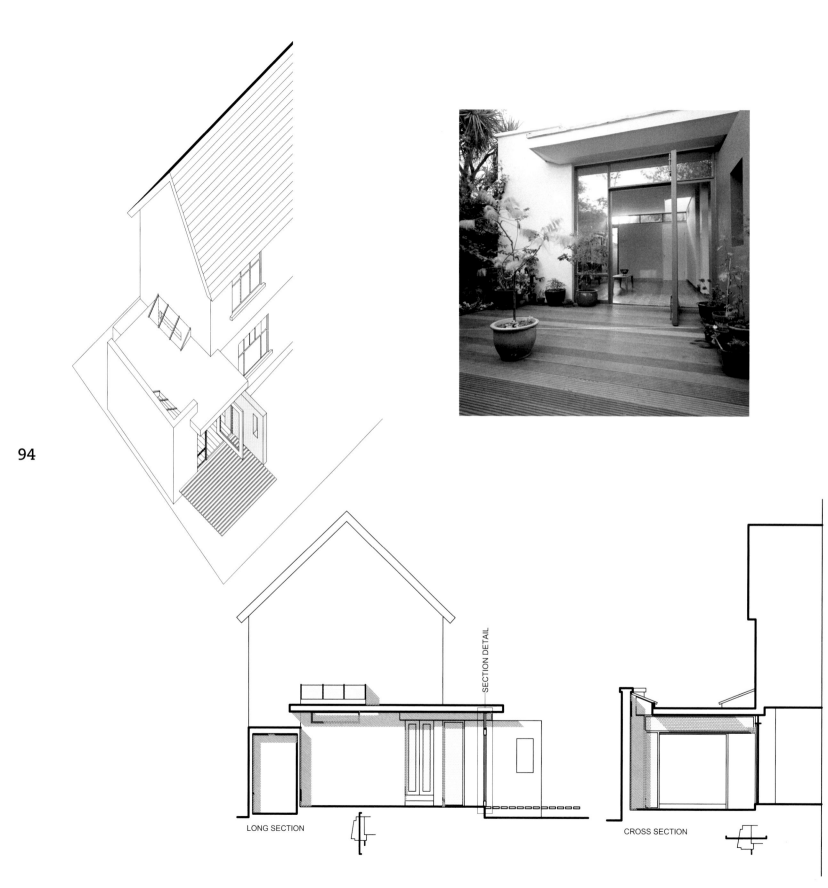

94

LONG SECTION

SECTION DETAIL

CROSS SECTION

The shell of a garage

95

Box Architecture

The owners of this home required additional living space. While the architects could have reconfigured internal rooms, there was an opportunity to incorporate an original garage, used over the years for storage rather than for cars.

The double garage, attached to the two-storey period home, was structurally sound. However, it needed additional light and a connection to the garden in order to convert it into a living area. "The scheme was driven by its relationship with nature. Making a physical link to the external environment was crucial to its success," says architect Paul Beckwith of Box Architecture.

The former garage was remodelled with rendered walls and highlight windows, and two new skylights were inserted into the roof. However, the most important element in the new living area is floor-to-ceiling glass windows and a large glass pivotal door that leads to an outdoor deck. The indoor/outdoor space is further strengthened by the projection of the horizontal plane of the ceiling beyond the enclosure and by the continuation of the floor plane to the exterior. "The opening of the pivotal door is an important element in the design," says Beckwith.

Box Architecture was also mindful of the positioning of planes and skylights to manipulate light penetration at different times of the day and in all seasons. The intention was to create awareness in the occupant of the nature of the path of light; the concept of a 'light time clock'.

Shifting the perspective

F2 Architecture

This large Victorian home was originally a gracious residence. However, for the best part of its life, it was used as a boarding house. More recently, it has been remodelled by F2 Architecture. The original rooms at the front of the house were fully restored. "We had to reinstate walls, floors and ceilings and completely redesign the 1970s addition," says architect Frank Marioli.

While the home's original arched Victorian windows were retained, a dramatic glass wall was inserted between the two connected rooms at the front, one intended to be used as an office, the other as a library. "Essentially, we wanted to change the perspective of the space as well as the scale of each room," says Marioli. "It's similar to hanging a piece of art and seeing how a room changes," he adds.

Instead of hanging a painting, F2 Architecture installed a series of panels made from low-iron glass, each 1.2 metres wide. The images on the panels, taken by photographer Chris Budgeon, were then transferred onto film and attached to the panels. The images capture the history of the area, which was once swampland. Budgeon photographed sand, shells and small coastal objects, before enlarging and digitally altering the images.

The glass panels are also used as a linking device to the new joinery in the library. Set apart from the windows by 200 millimetres, these panels create a different ambience depending on the time of day. "During the day, the glass is almost black and reflects corners and walls. But at night, backlit by neon tubes, the glass appears more animated," says Marioli.

The same technique was used at the top of the stairs. "The owner originally wanted a chandelier. The glass provides a contemporary interpretation," he adds.

JOINERY

Bathed in light

Perkins Architects

This large Federation-style home, built around the turn of the 19th century, has been completely renovated by Perkins Architects. "We retained most of the original rooms, but added a contemporary wing," says architect Ian Perkins, who was impressed with the scale and generous dimensions found in the original home.

To create the spacious new kitchen and informal living areas, a series of small box-like rooms – the scullery, laundry, kitchen and maid's room – were removed. "They weren't suited to a family with teenage children," says Perkins.

The new kitchen features MDF joinery with a low-sheen spray paint finish and overhead cupboards made of timber veneer. Perkins created a chequerboard effect by alternating the direction of the

grain with each cupboard door. To soften the effect of the timber against the white walls, fluorescent lights were inserted at the top and bottom of this joinery.

In contrast to the joinery, the pantry is completely open, with chunky MDF shelves on display. "The pantry is tucked away in one corner of the kitchen, so it's not visible," says Perkins, who did, however, finish the shelves with the same level of detail as if they were on display.

Perkins also designed shelving for the formal living area/study in the original part of the house. The floor-to-ceiling bookshelves feature a 'washed effect', with concealed lighting placed behind the centre shelves. "I wanted to give the shelves a traditional feel, but with a contemporary edge," says Perkins, who varied the distance between each shelf, as well as providing storage at the base of the shelves.

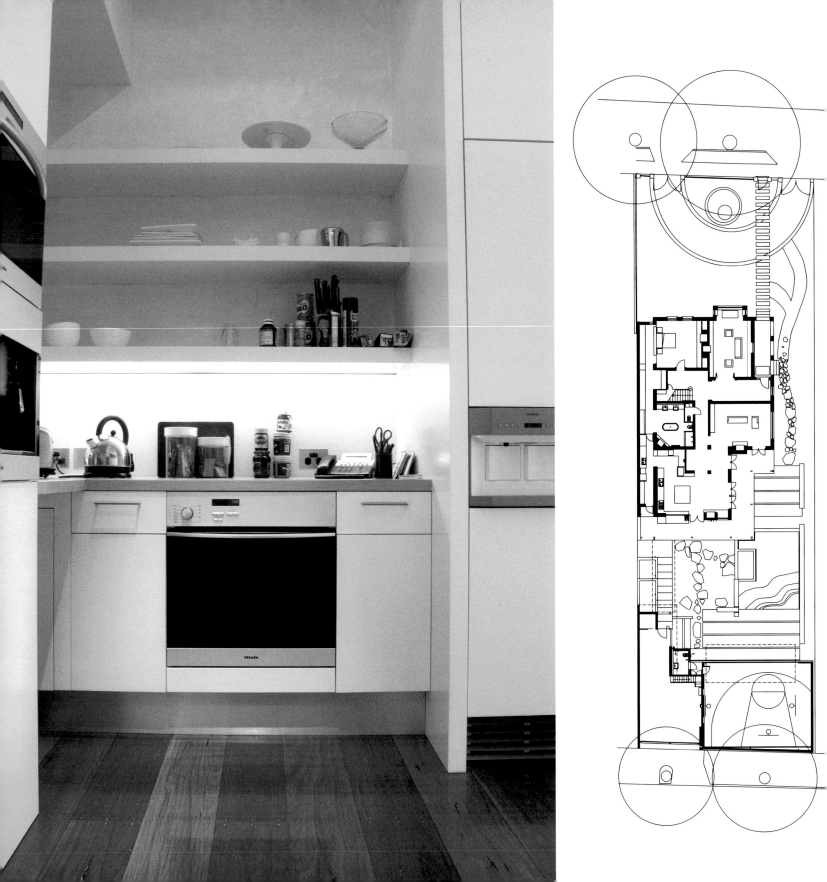

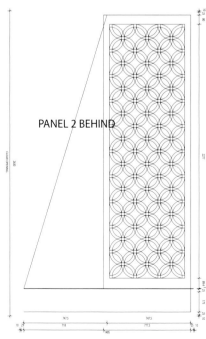

PANEL 2 BEHIND

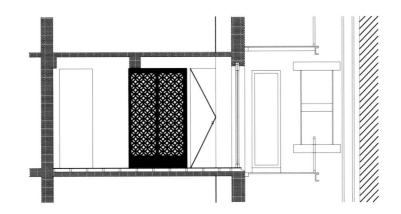

Decorative service box

Architect Fiona Winzar

107

Architect Fiona Winzar refers to the unusual joinery in her apartment as 'a decorative service box'. Located at the entrance to the spacious 1920s apartment, which she shares with her family, the 'box' adds a rich layer to the minimal white space. "The builder couldn't believe the level of detail. He thought a service cupboard should be simply clad with white doors, so it would completely disappear from view," says Winzar.

While massive beams and columns were retained in the renovation, nearly everything else was removed to create the three bedrooms, two bathrooms and open-plan living areas required. One addition was the service box at the entrance, which houses several utilities behind its decorative sliding doors. Immediately inside the front door are the hot water service and a narrow cupboard to hang coats. On the same side, facing the entrance is a separate cupboard that contains a washing machine and clothes dryer.

In a cupboard facing the open-plan kitchen and living area is a concealed bookshelf and cocktail cabinet. Screened by two sliding doors, a moiré effect is created when the two doors are left ajar. "It's probably the most used 'box' in the house. But it's not obvious," says Winzar, who had the veneer marine-ply screen doors 'routed' in a Moorish pattern that not only evokes the style of the apartment building, but also the local architecture. "The pattern was achieved through a computer program. But although technology was used, it was still a fairly intensive process," she adds. On the third side of the service box is a translucent sliding glass door that leads to the children's bathroom.

While the design is fairly minimal, the screen doors enclosing the service box add a rich layer to the space. As Winzar says, "I could have taken the builder's advice. It certainly would have been easier. But the effect clearly wouldn't have been the same".

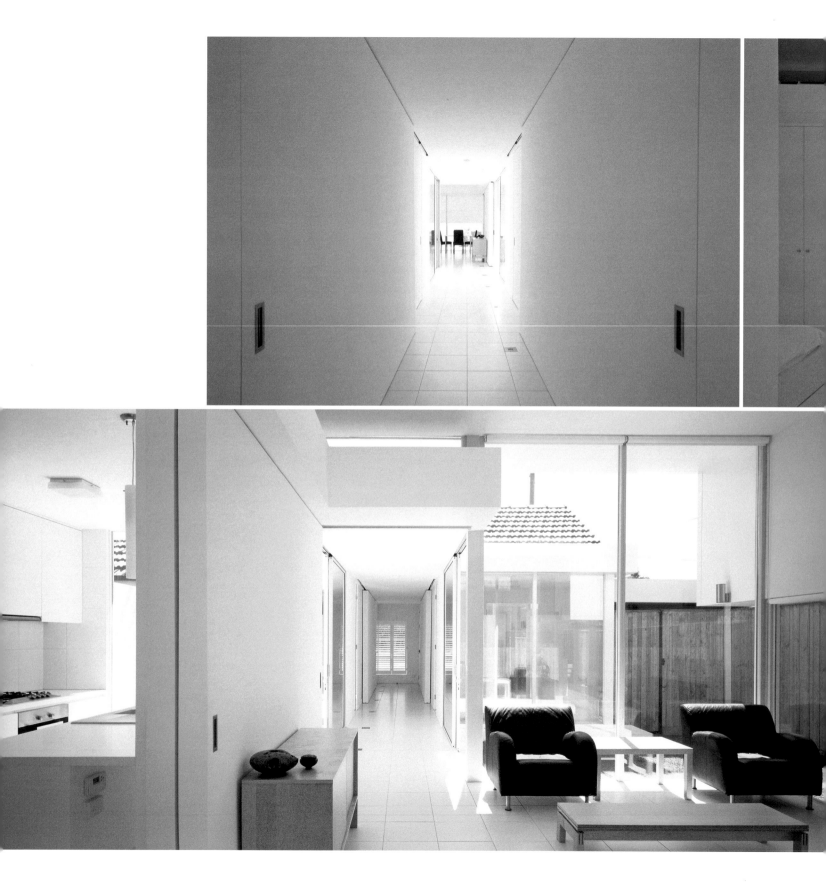

PHOTOGRAPHY: SHANIA SHEGEDYN

Flexible spaces

David Luck Architecture

This house was built by returned soldiers after the Second World War. "Most houses of the time were constructed as either one of two types, being single- or double-storey, with burnt brown brickwork, timber windows and a fired clay tile roof," says architect David Luck, who created a new contemporary home for the owners.

The house's original layout of rooms was inadequate for contemporary living. Living areas were cramped, a single bedroom had no wardrobe space or direct access to a bathroom and the kitchen was small and marginalised along a wall beside a back door. "Demolishing the entire interior allowed us to excavate the roof space for storage and a mezzanine music room," says Luck.

One of the most striking aspects of the renovation was the insertion of thick sliding walls, used to define the kitchen and living areas or the bedrooms and ensuites. "The use of sliding doors/walls allowed us to create a universal space that meets a combination of potential dwelling spaces that could cater for an older couple, a single-parent family, a couple, or single homeowners that may have friends or family stay for the short or longer term," says Luck.

The doors/walls, made of steel studwork and plaster, frame the main passage leading to the living areas. The doors can be pulled back to reveal two bedrooms opposite each other. "The owners might want to create one large bedroom or divide the space into two bedrooms. Flexibility was part of the brief," says Luck, who also created the same flexibility in the open-plan living areas. "The kitchen can be closed off completely or alternatively, one side can be revealed. And if the owners entertain, the entire space can be opened up," says Luck, pointing out the different views achieved, depending on the position of the walls/doors.

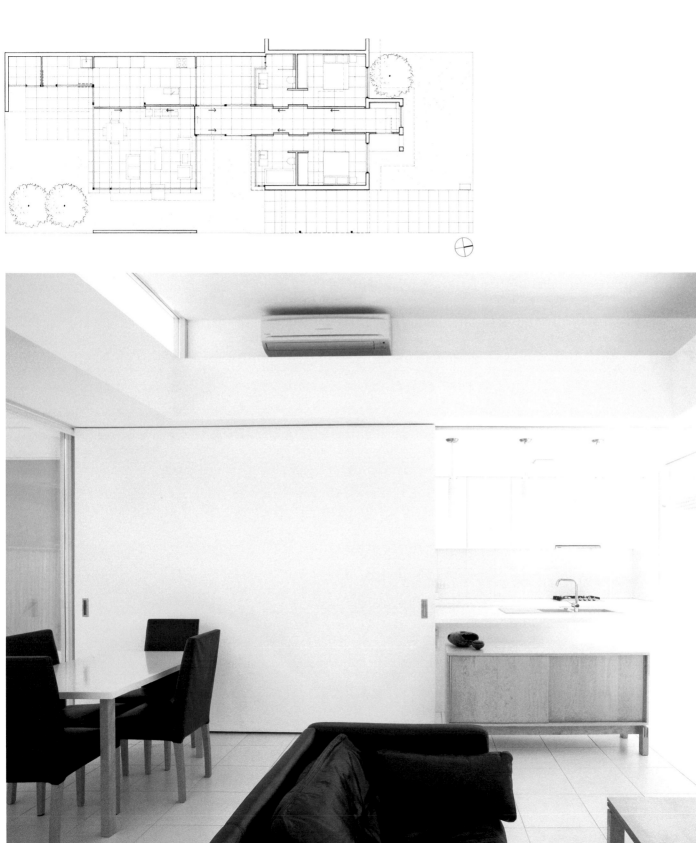

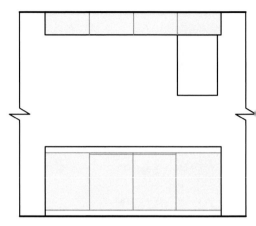

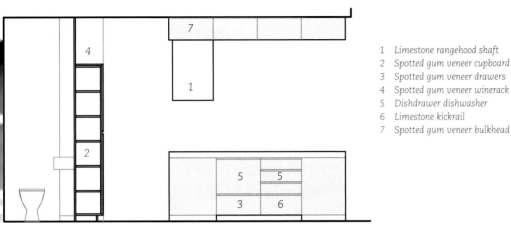

1 Limestone rangehood shaft
2 Spotted gum veneer cupboard
3 Spotted gum veneer drawers
4 Spotted gum veneer winerack
5 Dishdrawer dishwasher
6 Limestone kickrail
7 Spotted gum veneer bulkhead

Hub of the house

Alsocan Architecture

115

The edge of the kitchen bench is visible immediately past the front door. "The bench almost leads you into the hub of the house," says architect Jane McDougall. Like the spacious three-storey inner-city house, the kitchen bench is generous in proportion, measuring 2.7 by 2.7 metres.

As the kitchen is located at the centre of the open-plan living areas, the architects were keen to ensure the joinery was well integrated. Featuring a limestone benchtop and spotted gum timber veneer cupboards below, the central island bench is the place to congregate. "We designed the bench to allow the owner to prepare a meal on one side and guests to enjoy drinks on the other side," says McDougall.

As the bench is extremely wide, a sandblasted glass plate was inserted in the centre of the limestone. Backlit by a halogen light, the glass panel provides extra light and enhances objects on display. Power points appear on each side of the glass to allow for the use of electric appliances. A limestone rangehood was also designed above the bench. "We were playing with the idea of the cube. We wanted it to appear as simply an object in the kitchen rather than something purely utilitarian," says McDougall.

While the central bench appears relatively homogenous on all four sides, there are certain details that relate to function. For example, limestone kickboards only appear on the non-cooking side of the bench. "We wanted to give more leg room to the chef while preparing a meal," she says.

The central bench provides an important focus of the kitchen as well to the living areas. And although there are comfortable lounges to one side of the bench, guests invariably stand at the bench. As McDougall says, "People love watching food being prepared. It's an instinctive reaction that's universal".

PHOTOGRAPHY: JOHN GOLLINGS

Industrial aesthetic

117

Architects EAT

This home was originally a printing factory. Converted by Architects EAT, the building was completely reworked. The kitchen, which is on the first floor together with a bathroom, ensuite and two bedrooms, is connected to the open-plan living areas and looks out to a light-filled courtyard.

The kitchen features bright red joinery with two-pack MDF cupboards. Also included in the joinery are gloss white vinyl doors that conceal the fridge, pantry and laundry. Acrylic also appears as the finish of the central island bench. "The kitchen joinery has quite a plasticised feel. We wanted that sense of plasticity to also feature in the façade," says architect Albert Mo.

As a contrast to the red-lacquered joinery, the architects created a bulkhead over the large centre island bench (measuring 2.5 by 1.5 metres). Made of zinc tiles, the canopy defines the cooking areas as

well as providing an interesting juxtaposition of materials. "We had to allow air to circulate behind the tiles. Zinc needs to be able to breathe," says Mo. The zinc canopy also conceals structural elements that support the roof-top terrace directly above the kitchen.

While the acrylic materials naturally reflect the sunlight during the day, artificial lighting activates the kitchen at night. A fluorescent tube, encased in stainless steel, hovers above the central island bench and can be adjusted either up or down to suit the owner's requirements. An incandescent light tube has also been inserted into the central bench. Positioned facing the living area, this embedded light makes the space glow.

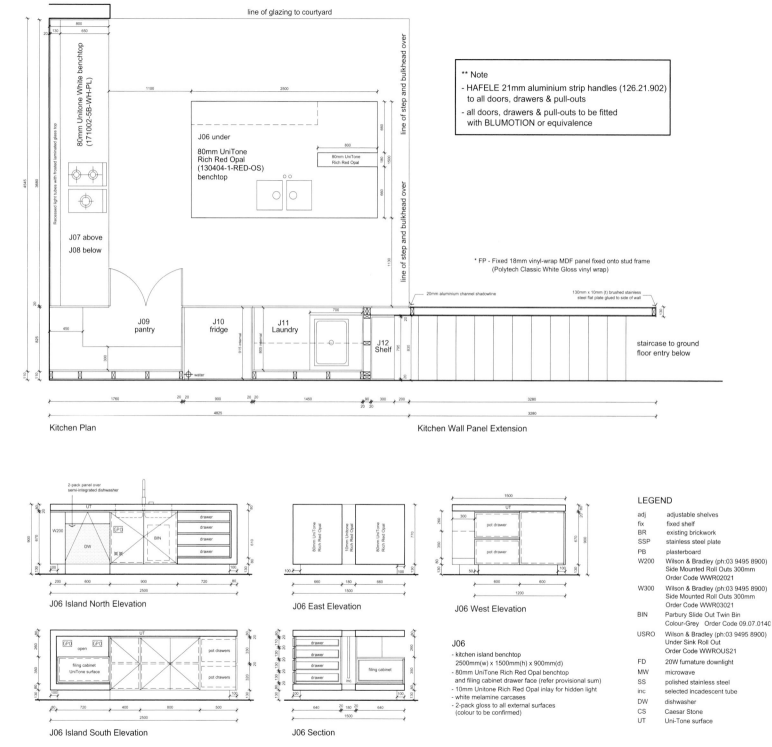

line of glazing to courtyard

Note
- HAFELE 21mm aluminium strip handles (126.21.902) to all doors, drawers & pull-outs
- all doors, drawers & pull-outs to be fitted with BLUMOTION or equivalence

80mm Unitone White benchtop (171002-5B-WH-PL)

Recessed light tubes with frosted laminated glass top

J06 under
80mm UniTone Rich Red Opal (130404-1-RED-OS) benchtop

80mm UniTone Rich Red Opal

J07 above
J08 below

line of step and bulkhead over

* FP - Fixed 18mm vinyl-wrap MDF panel fixed onto stud frame (Polytech Classic White Gloss vinyl wrap)

20mm aluminium channel shadowline

130mm x 10mm (t) brushed stainless steel flat plate glued to side of wall

J09 pantry

J10 fridge

J11 Laundry

J12 Shelf

water

staircase to ground floor entry below

118

Kitchen Plan

Kitchen Wall Panel Extension

2-pack panel over semi-integrated dishwasher

UT
W200
GPO
DW
BIN
drawer
drawer
drawer
drawer

J06 Island North Elevation

UT
80mm UniTone Rich Red Opal
10mm Unitone Rich Red Opal
80mm UniTone Rich Red Opal

J06 East Elevation

UT
pot drawer
pot drawer

J06 West Elevation

GPO GPO
open
filing cabinet UniTone surface
pot drawers
pot drawers

J06 Island South Elevation

drawer
drawer
drawer
drawer
filing cabinet
inc.

J06 Section

J06
- kitchen island benchtop
  2500mm(w) x 1500mm(h) x 900mm(d)
- 80mm UniTone Rich Red Opal benchtop
  and filing cabinet drawer face (refer provisional sum)
- 10mm Unitone Rich Red Opal inlay for hidden light
- white melamine carcases
- 2-pack gloss to all external surfaces
  (colour to be confirmed)

LEGEND

adj	adjustable shelves
fix	fixed shelf
BR	existing brickwork
SSP	stainless steel plate
PB	plasterboard
W200	Wilson & Bradley (ph:03 9495 8900) Side Mounted Roll Outs 300mm Order Code WWR02021
W300	Wilson & Bradley (ph:03 9495 8900) Side Mounted Roll Outs 300mm Order Code WWR03021
BIN	Parbury Slide Out Twin Bin Colour-Grey Order Code 09.07.0140
USRO	Wilson & Bradley (ph:03 9495 8900) Under Sink Roll Out Order Code WWROUS21
FD	20W furnature downlight
MW	microwave
SS	polished stainless steel
inc	selected incadescent tube
DW	dishwasher
CS	Caesar Stone
UT	Uni-Tone surface

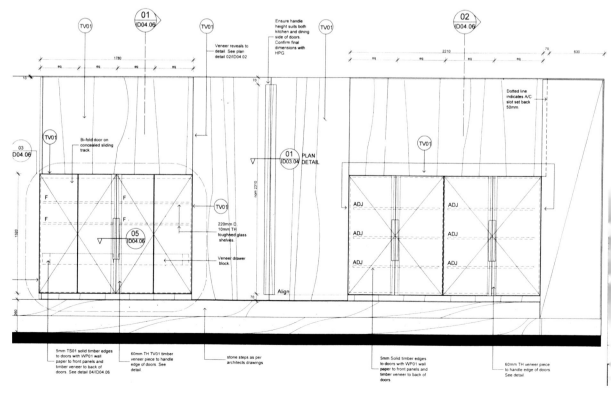

TV01   01   ID04.06   TV01

Ensure handle
height suits both
kitchen and dining
side of doors.
Confirm final
dimensions with
HPG

Veneer reveals to
detail. See plan
detail 02/ID04.02

TV01   02   ID04.06

1780

eq   eq   eq   eq

70

2210   70   630

eq   eq   eq   eq

Dotted line
indicates A/C
slot set back
50mm.

03
ID04.06

TV01

Bi-fold door on
concealed sliding
track.

01
ID03.04

PLAN
DETAIL

TV01

nom 2310

F   F

F   F

1320

05
ID04.06

220mm D
10mm TH
toughened glass
shelves

TV01

Veneer drawer
block

Align

70

ADJ   ADJ

ADJ   ADJ

ADJ   ADJ

5mm TS01 solid timber edges
to doors with WP01 wall
paper to front panels and
timber veneer to back of
doors. See detail 04/ID04.06

60mm TH TV01 timber
veneer piece to handle
edge of doors. See
detail.

stone steps as per
architects drawings

5mm Solid timber edges
to doors with WP01 wall
paper to front panels and
timber veneer to back of
doors

60mm TH veneer piece
to handle edge of doors.
See detail

Integral detailing

121

BURO Architects in association with Hecker Phelan & Guthrie Interiors

This large Victorian home was completed remodelled by BURO Architects, Hecker Phelan & Guthrie and London-based architect Hugh Tuffley. The three practices collaborated on both the design and joinery. "We worked closely together. The interior detailing is integral to the architecture," says architect Stephen Javens of BURO Architects.

A new open-plan kitchen, dining and living area was added to the rear of the home, with a main bedroom suite located directly above. The new wing commences at the end of the main corridor with an office, lined in stained American oak. "We removed a wall where the desk is," says Javens, who was keen to fuse the original home with the new addition.

Head-height cupboards, covered in rough silk, extend across the kitchen and dining area. Framed in American oak and lined with a yellowish-tinged acid glass, these striking cupboards include a cocktail cabinet as well as drawers for crockery and general storage. "We wanted to thicken the walls between the formal dining and the casual living areas," says Javens. An American oak sliding door between the two spaces was also included in the design.

When the cupboards are closed, they create a golden and tactile canvas across the living areas, appearing as part of the back wall. And when the cocktail cabinet is opened, there's a wonderful hue cast across the space. "Our clients entertain a lot, so these cupboards were an important part of the design. These cupboards also free up the dining area. There's a credenza, but the space isn't cluttered up with unnecessary joinery," adds Javens.

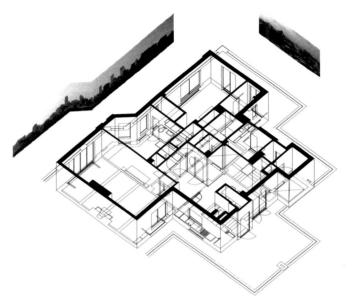

Jigsaw puzzle
aardvarchitecture

This penthouse, situated on the edge of Central Park, New York, is surrounded by extraordinary uninterrupted views. According to architects Lynette Widder and Christian Volkmann, the challenge of the project was to develop strategies at the small scale of details, which would create continuity with the large scale of those deep urban views.

The interior organisation of rooms in the 1920s building was efficient and intelligent. It also had the potential to offer spatial continuity through the apartment along oblique view lines. The façade openings and the existing windows, however, did little to extend those view lines out towards the surrounding skyline. Therefore, all interventions were concentrated on resolving this problem.

One of the most effective solutions was the reconfiguration of the ensuite to the main bedroom. Originally this space was separated from the terrace by a wardrobe. This wardrobe was removed and a new opening was cut into the brick cavity wall. The bathtub was then positioned immediately next to the new window, allowing a dialogue between interior space, terrace and skyline.

The bathroom, including the bathtub and shower basin, was prefabricated in Germany using a unique CNC milling process, then shipped to New York in jigsaw puzzle-like pieces and installed over two days. The relationship between interior and exterior was further articulated in the design with the built-in furniture on the terrace. "These teak and cedar built-ins create a datum that appears on both sides of the wall," says Widder, referring to the timber planter boxes that conceal an irrigation system, lighting and outdoor speakers.

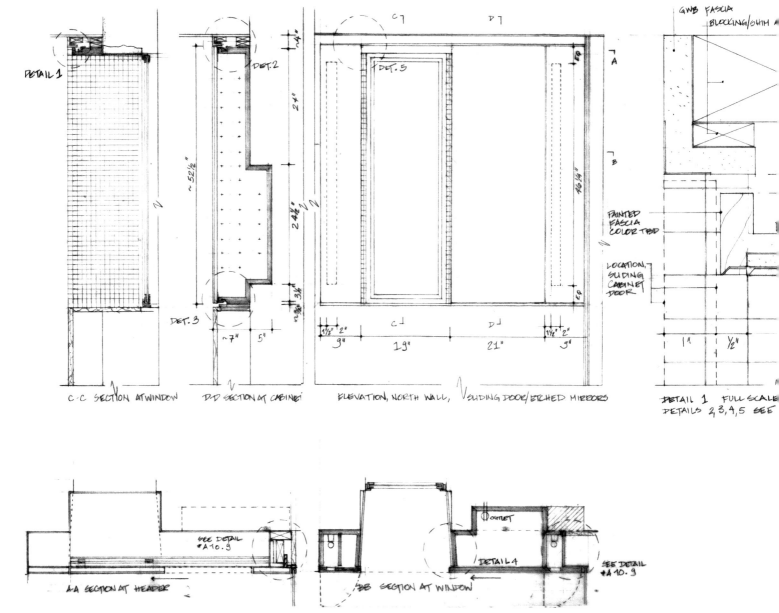

126

DETAIL 1

DET. 2

DET. 3

~52½"

24"

24½"

~7" 5"

C-C SECTION AT WINDOW

D-D SECTION AT CABINET

C 7   D 7

DET. 5

A

B

46¼"

EQ

EQ

PAINTED
FASCIA
COLOR TBD

LOCATION,
SLIDING
CABINET
DOOR

1½" 2"
9"

C ⌐

19"

D ⌐

21"

1½" 2"
9"

ELEVATION, NORTH WALL, SLIDING DOOR/ETCHED MIRRORS

GWB FASCIA
BLOCKING/SHIM

1" ½"

DETAIL 1   FULL SCALE
DETAILS 2,3,4,5 SEE

SEE DETAIL
#A 10.9

A-A SECTION AT HEADER

OUTLET

DETAIL 4

SEE DETAIL
#A 10.9

B-B SECTION AT WINDOW

405.55.011
CABINET HEADER

¼" CONCRETE BOARD
GLASS MOSAIC, ¾"

~3½"

1"

¾"

¼"

³∕₁₆"

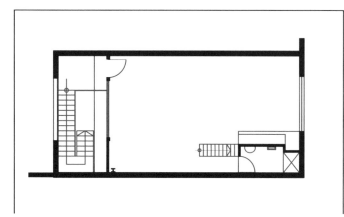

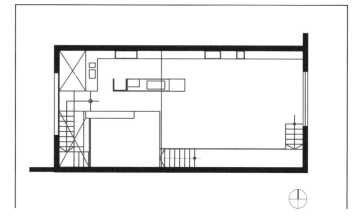

Limited space

Multiplicity

129

This kitchen occupies a linear space on the first floor of a narrow multi-storey warehouse. "We were restricted by the width of the kitchen," says architect Tim O'Sullivan, who was able to create a workable environment with a distance of just 0.9 metres between the kitchen joinery and the central island bench. "It's reasonably tight, particularly as both of the owners enjoy cooking," he adds.

The architects used 'onboard' gloss white laminate for the kitchen cupboards, for its economy and for its light-reflecting qualities. To create a feeling of openness, there are as few barriers as possible. Traditional cupboard handles were dispensed with – extruded aluminium edges on each cupboard are used instead. "The kitchen really 'bleeds' into the living area," says O'Sullivan's partner, Sioux Clark, referring to the way the kitchen joinery extends into the living area to provide extra storage and display objects. An apple-green 'cube' placed between the joinery in the living room activates the space and forms a certain delineation between the kitchen and living areas.

Concrete is used on the island bench and stainless steel features on the remaining kitchen benches. A dropped ceiling over the kitchen also helps define this area. "We wanted to create a sense of arrival when you reach the top of the stairs. It's quite a simple kitchen, but it's extremely functional," says O'Sullivan.

PHOTOGRAPHY: MARK SMITH

Over the threshold

133

Stevens Lawson Architects

This house, designed by Nicholas Stevens and Gary Lawson, is a landmark in the area of Herne Bay, Auckland, New Zealand. The front door to the two-storey house is as striking as the façade, which is made of glass-reinforced concrete and features a triangular-shaped pattern, reminiscent of Tapa motifs found in the Pacific islands.

The front door, like the living areas on the ground floor, is reasonably transparent. To maintain privacy, the architects included a high front fence in the design. "But we wanted to give something back to the street," says Stevens, referring to the sculptural façade that enlivens both this house and the inner-city streetscape.

The large pivoting front door takes its cue from the triangular concrete façade. The door, measuring 2 metres wide by 2.7 metres high, also features triangular-shaped timber battens set in clear toughened glass. The cedar door has been stained a dark ebony colour and offers a complete view of the hallway, which is terminated by a bright scarlet curtain.

A 2.7-metre-high handle on the front door is detailed with several cut-out shapes to assist opening. As a result, the door can be opened by people of varying heights. "Cedar is a relatively light material. And because the door is pivotal, it's even lighter," says Stevens, who lined the hallway with honed concrete blocks. "There's quite a lot of timber and concrete in the house. So it was appropriate to include a timber front door," adds Stevens, who angled the front door's timber battens in several directions to give it animation, like the façade.

Playful extension

Nicholas Gioia Associates

Architect Nicholas Gioia created a sense of playfulness in this extension to a double-fronted Victorian house. While the original front rooms were restored in a traditional way, the extension contains an element of surprise. "I wanted to create a sense of freedom as you enter the new wing," says Gioia, who added a new kitchen, dining and living area, together with a mezzanine that functions as a second living area or as an office.

Gioia kept the palette of materials fairly minimal. The kitchen features Carrara marble benchtops and two-pack polyurethane MDF joinery, all in white. The kitchen bench was used to separate the kitchen from the dining area and appears to 'float' in the space. "The idea was to increase the sense of space rather than anchoring every piece of joinery to the floor," says Gioia.

One piece of joinery that is firmly anchored is the 4.5-metre-high pillar. Made of Victorian ash veneer and stained a dark chocolate brown to complement the timber floors, it has three separate functions. On the kitchen side, it contains the pantry and a microwave recess. On the dining area side, there's an alcove for displaying glass as well as a cupboard for storing cutlery and crockery. And on the mezzanine level, where the pillar protrudes, there's an additional cupboard.

In the dining area, two units, also made of two-pack polyurethane and timber veneer, appear to float across a translucent glass window. The shelves and cupboards are used for storage and also house the stereo system and speakers. And while the shelves in the dining area activate the interior, their silhouette also energises a side laneway at night.

SECTIONS

RICHARDSON HOUSE
NICHOLAS MURRAY ARCHITECTS

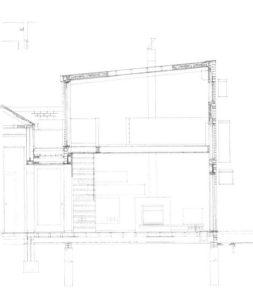

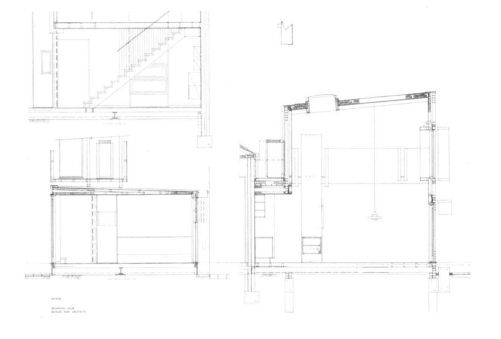

SECTIONS

RICHARDSON HOUSE
NICHOLAS SIKA ARCHITECTS

139

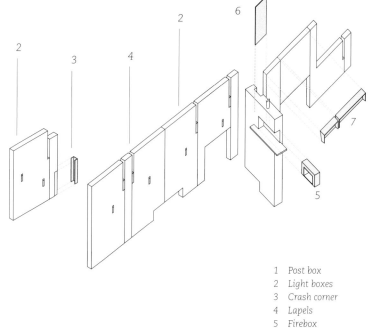

1 Post box
2 Light boxes
3 Crash corner
4 Lapels
5 Firebox
6 Lazarus door
7 Robe

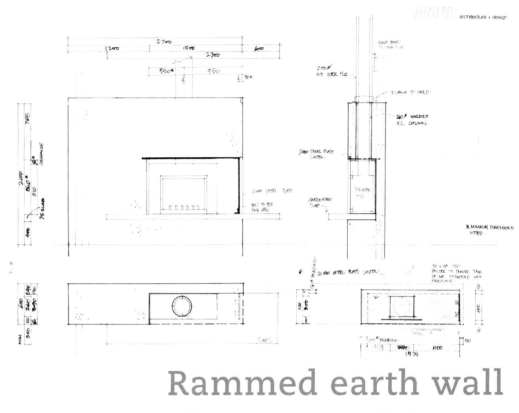

Rammed earth wall

141

Phorm Architecture + Design

This Queensland house features several materials, including a rammed earth wall. "We were conscious of expressing the rammed earth, both externally and internally," says architect Paul Hotston.

The rammed earth wall is a highlight of the main bedroom. While the wall adds texture and warmth to the bedroom, the architects were also mindful of the need to provide wardrobe space. "We didn't want to cover up the rammed earth with cupboards. So we used powder-coated steel as clothing racks and left them exposed," says Hotston, referring to the way the hanging shirts become part of the feature wall. Beneath the shirts are six metal-coated shoe racks to complement the clothes racks. "We refer to this wardrobe as a 'prêt-à-porter' robe. It's like going into a store and seeing everything on display," he adds.

The metal detailing used on all the rammed earth walls within the house provided a contemporary junction between the earth, a more ancient material, and the new. A copper-clad sliding door also appears in the bedroom and slides along the rammed earth wall. Seven folded copper lights inserted into the bottom of the earth wall illuminate the children's area. "At night, these lights are left on. They light a path for the children in case they need to reach their parents during the night," says Hotston.

143

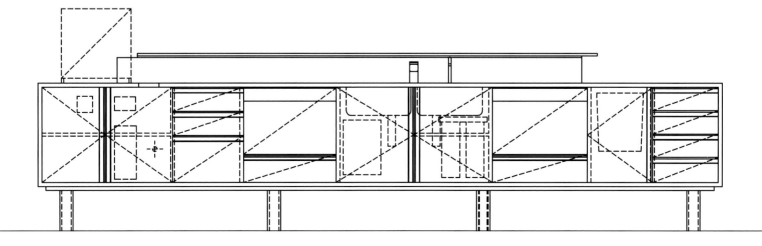

A rich palette of materials

Maddison Architects

The architects were approached by their clients to re-plan a substantial 1970's solid masonry home. The original layout consisted of a number of smaller rooms connected by narrow doorways. "We consolidated three rooms in the western wing of the U-shaped floor plan house to create one spacious open-plan kitchen, meals and living area," says architect Peter Maddison.

This new space is now the hub of the family home. Part of the architect's brief included a generous kitchen area with a semi-commercial stove and coffee machine. Shelving space for the owner's collection of antique model aeroplanes and other special objects was also required.

The architects developed one continuous wall unit through the space. Starting at one end as a bench seat, it becomes a kitchen bench and then extends into a laundry. The unifying element in

the space was strengthened by a bulkhead, which spears through an overhead glass highlight window into the laundry. The elongated forms of the wall unit, kitchen island bench, bamboo bar top and overhead cupboards visually appear to slide past one another within the confines of the space.

The materials used for the renovation resonate with the original style of the dwelling and are drawn from a rich palette. Amber-coloured glass mosaic tiles are used as splashbacks in both the kitchen and laundry. Laminated bamboo planks are used for the flooring, kitchen island bench bar top, and in a toothed application on the feature wall. Padded vinyl appears on the front of the bar. »

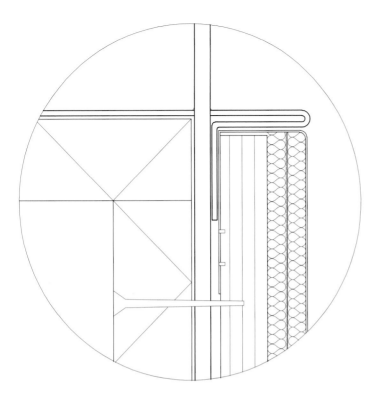

146 Maddison was also keen to create a sense of 'floating' in the kitchen. As a result, the kitchen benches, including the central island unit, are elevated above the floor. "It's much more of a challenge when you take this approach. All the services have to be perfectly aligned from the start of the project. There's no room for error. It's a more rigid design to accommodate", he explains.

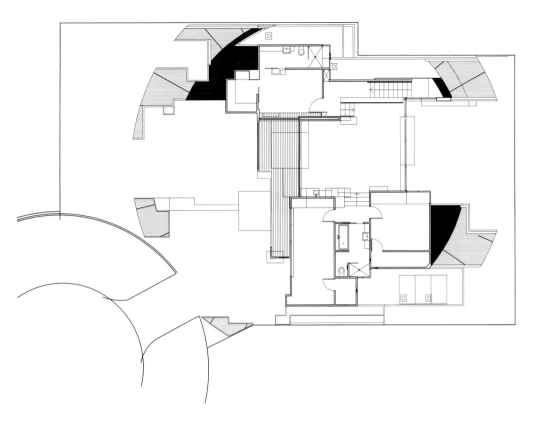

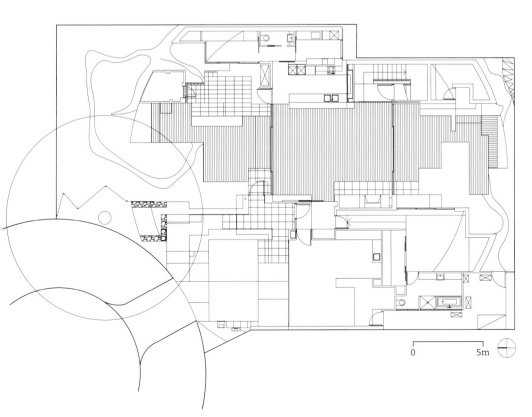

0   5m

PHOTOGRAPHY: JOHN GOLLINGS

Stacked boxes

McBride Charles Ryan Architecture + Interior Design

This unusual home is as explosive inside as outside. "The design is a bit like a puzzle that's been pulled apart," says Debbie-Lyn Ryan, interior designer and a director of the architecture and interior design practice.

The fine joinery is one of the many strengths of this home. Purple cupboards, spray-painted in a lustrous duco similar to a car finish, form the entrance. Used to hang coats, umbrellas and even photo albums, these cupboards extend the length of the hallway that leads to a bedroom and bathroom on a lower level. A sliding door, made of MDF and painted pale mauve, separates the entrance from the open-plan kitchen, dining and living areas. This door, which features a cut-out in the MDF rather than a traditional handle, can be pulled back into a wall cavity or closed for privacy.

As a contrast to the MDF joinery, spotted gum veneer is used for the cupboards in the dining area. Appearing as a series of 'stacked boxes', these cupboards appear to 'bleed' into the timber bulkhead directly above. "Some of the materials used in the joinery also appear on the exterior. The idea was to blur the division between the indoors and outdoors," says Ryan.

An oak tree in the garden has inspired the interior colour scheme. A variety of greens appear on the MDF sliding door that separates the living area from the staircase to the first-floor living area and bedrooms. While the joinery at ground level is about connecting to the garden, the joinery units in the kitchenette/living area on the first floor are pixels within the dome. Supporting a television set, as well as concealing a bar fridge, this joinery appears to float into the ceiling space. "Some of these lower cupboards are functional. The higher ones are made of plaster to suggest pixels," says Ryan, who feels that the part can often be more intriguing than the whole.

PHOTOGRAPHY: SCOTT HENDERSON, ERIC SIERINS

Three kitchens

Fitzpatrick + Partners

This new house, designed by James Fitzpatrick, includes three interconnecting kitchens. "The owners tend to cook a lot with oil. They didn't want the smells to go though the house," explains Fitzpatrick.

As the kitchen connects to the living areas of the house, Fitzpatrick used a minimal design with a limited palette of materials. Caesar stone was used on all the bench tops and polyurethane kitchen cupboards are mushroom coloured, as is the glass splashback that runs across the galley-style kitchen.

The 'cooking' kitchen can be concealed with a door leading into the main kitchen area. This kitchen includes commercial cooking appliances together with stainless steel benches and sinks that can be easily washed down.

The galley kitchen that runs along one wall was conceived as the service and preparation area. Large timber-stained doors that 'intersect' the stone bench conceal the microwave and double oven. As this area of the kitchen is well lit by skylights, Fitzpatrick was keen to deflect any glare from above. "The bulkhead over the bench also creates a more intimate space," he adds.

The third area of the kitchen was primarily designed for the young children who live in the house. This area includes a bench and stools as well as stained timber cupboards that contain the fridge, a pantry and storage areas. As Fitzpatrick says, "the owners call this area the 'dessert and coffee kitchen', and it always smells great".

153

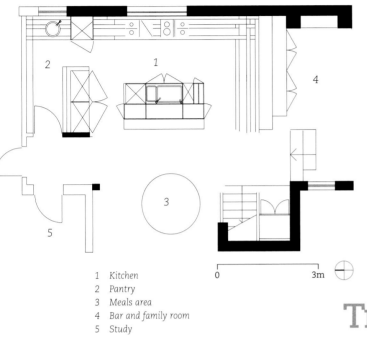

1   Kitchen
2   Pantry
3   Meals area
4   Bar and family room
5   Study

0   3m

Transformed by timber

Stephen Jolson Architect Pty Ltd

This kitchen appears as though timber has been bought into the home and carefully stacked to form the joinery – and it was. "Our client wanted the feel of a country-style kitchen. It's not a style that our practice is known for," says architect Stephen Jolson, who nevertheless was keen to pursue the project.

Large planks of spotted gum were sourced from a recycling yard. "The timber is about 180 years old," says Jolson, who worked closely with a boat builder in creating the kitchen joinery. "The boat builder understood the importance of the timber and is accustomed to creating fine detail," he adds.

As the timber was brought into the home, it was carefully stacked and transformed into kitchen joinery, with the ends of each length cheekily protruding at one end. "We wanted to celebrate the timber, with all its imperfections, rather than mask them," says Jolson, who

created an L-shaped design for the cupboards. These cupboards extend at one end of the kitchen to form a pantry area. This area is made of stainless steel rather than timber; the change in materials defines the functions within the kitchen.

The island bench in the centre of the kitchen is also made of a different material. Featuring a limestone benchtop and painted MDF cupboards below, the island bench acts as a 'workhorse'. Many of the appliances, including the dishwasher, are concealed behind the cupboard doors.

While the new kitchen isn't exactly the country-style kitchen initially conceived by the owners, it does show a level of detail sometimes missing in contemporary design. With its 'feathered' ends, the timber is seen for what it is, with fine grain and subtle variations in colour between the various lengths.

157

FIREPLACES

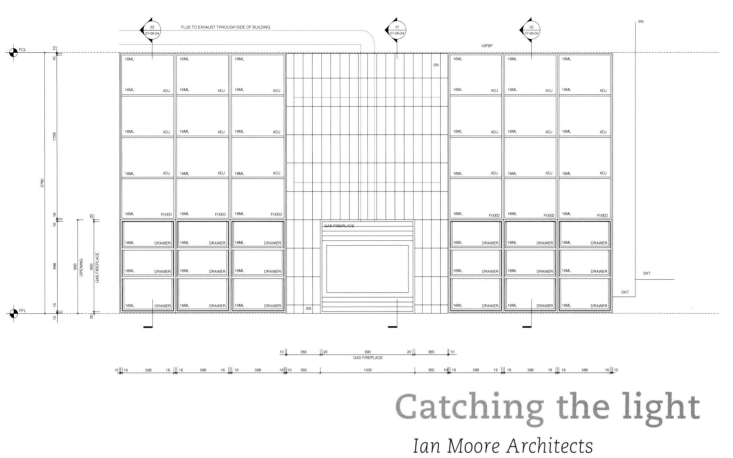

Catching the light

Ian Moore Architects

This spacious family home overlooks Balmoral Beach in Mosman, Sydney. As the site is relatively steep, the house appears considerably larger from the rear elevation. Conceived as two separate pavilions linked by a large staircase, the 350-square-metre house cascades down the site over four levels.

The house features two living areas on the lowest level. On one side of the descending staircase is the open-plan kitchen, dining and living area. The more formal living area, complete with fireplace, is on the other side. Both of these living spaces connect to a large timber deck that affords impressive views over Middle Harbour.

The formal living area features a Jetmaster fireplace surrounded by 'flamed' basalt wall tiles. This fireplace is flush with the American oak joinery that was designed to contain a music system, drawers for CDs and videos, and general storage. Basalt tiles also appear on the living room floors, but this honed basalt, known as 'Cubana', provides a smoother finish than the slightly rougher texture used to frame the fireplace. "When the light streams in, the flamed basalt catches the light from every angle. Sometimes, you can identify at least ten different shades of grey. There's a resemblance to subtle patchwork," says architect Ian Moore. "I was also keen to add texture to the design," he adds.

The focus is on the fireplace during the cooler months, but underfloor heating is also used. The fireplace is often used even when the large glass sliding doors to the deck are opened, taking the chill out of the air both in the living area and on the terrace.

The focal point
de Campo Architects

Architect Chris de Campo speaks passionately about the fireplace. "It means home, heart, warmth and survival among other things. It was also one of the early links to creating shelter". In Victorian times, the fireplace was the focal point of the home, with women protecting themselves with a fan to ensure a pale complexion.

Fast forward to the 21st century, the fireplace is still regarded as an important element in the home. Chris de Campo's own home, which he shares with his wife, interior designer Genevieve de Campo and their children, features an unusual disc-like fireplace in the living room of the house. As in Victorian times, this fireplace is the focal point of the three-storey home.

Positioned 200 millimetres from the entry's floor-to-ceiling windows, the fireplace greets visitors upon arrival. Set on a concrete plinth

that extends to the front door, the fireplace, designed by the de Campos, takes the form of a steel disc and flue, painted in fire-resistant silver paint. The wood-burning fireplace channels heat throughout the ground floor. "The house was built on a concrete slab, so the heat is channelled across the living areas. There's also heating set into the concrete floor," says de Campo, who refers to the front living area as the 'everything room'. "It's where the children play. And it's also used by us to entertain friends," he adds.

This fireplace was conceived as a freestanding object rather than set into a wall. "It was seen as a centrepiece in the design of the house. It's not just the aesthetics that please us, it's also the sound of burning wood and the flicker of light against walls. It's extremely soothing," says de Campo.

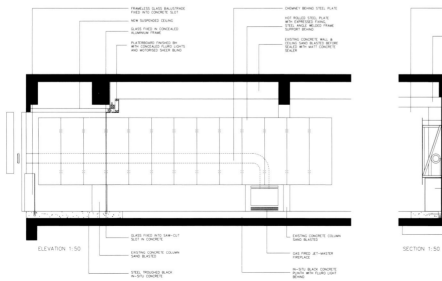

FRAMELESS GLASS BALUSTRADE
FIXED INTO CONCRETE SLOT

NEW SUSPENDED CEILING

GLASS FIXED IN CONCEALED
ALUMINIUM FRAME

PLATERBOARD FINISHED BH
WITH CONCEALED FLURO LIGHTS
AND MOTORISED SHEER BLIND

CHEMNEY BEHIND STEEL PLATE

HOT ROLLED STEEL PLATE
WITH EXPRESSED FIXING,
STEEL ANGLE WELDED FRAME
SUPPORT BEHIND

EXISTING CONCRETE WALL &
CEILING SAND BLASTED BEFORE
SEALED WITH MATT CONCRETE
SEALER

GLASS FIXED INTO SAW-CUT
SLOT IN CONCRETE

EXISTING CONCRETE COLUMN
SAND BLASTED

STEEL TROUGHED BLACK
IN-SITU CONCRETE

EXISTING CONCRETE COLUMN
SAND BLASTED

GAS FIRED JET-MASTER
FIREPLACE

IN-SITU BLACK CONCRETE
PLINTH WITH FLURO LIGHT
BEHIND

ELEVATION 1:50

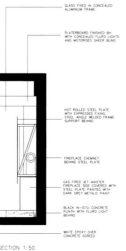

GLASS FIXED IN CONCEALED
ALUMINIUM FRAME

PLATERBOARD FINISHED BH
WITH CONCEALED FLURO LIGHTS
AND MOTORISED SHEER BLIND

HOT ROLLED STEEL PLATE
WITH EXPRESSED FIXING,
STEEL ANGLE WELDED FRAME
SUPPORT BEHIND

FIREPLACE CHEMNEY
BEHIND STEEL PLATE

GAS FIRED JET-MASTER
FIREPLACE SIDE COVERED WITH
STEEL PLATE PAINTED WITH
DARK GREY METALIC PAINT

BLACK IN-SITU CONCRETE
PLINTH WITH FLURO LIGHT
BEHIND

WHITE EPOXY OVER
CONCRETE SCREED

SECTION 1:50

Like a painting

Architect Greg Gong

This fireplace is located in a large open-plan living area, in an apartment in West Melbourne. Purchased as a shell, the 220-square-metre warehouse was converted into a three-bedroom home by architect Greg Gong. "The owners wanted something that had an industrial aesthetic. But a place that felt like a home," says Gong, who sees the fireplace as a significant symbol of domesticity.

The open-plan living areas in this apartment feature massive beams on both walls and ceiling. While Gong was content to express the beams, he wanted to conceal the flue to the Jetmaster gas fireplace. To achieve this, he used 13 hot rolled steel panels that are supported from the wall by a steel beam. Measuring 7 metres long by 1.5 metres wide, the panels not only conceal the flue, but act as a piece of artwork.

"People normally avoid using hot rolled steel, because of the imperfections that are created. But the burn marks are like birth marks – they're part of life," says Gong, who suspended the panels 550 millimetres from the wall. The panels extend beyond the glass windows in the living area. "I didn't want to create a barrier to the balcony. The indoor and outdoor areas appear as one," he adds.

While the fireplace sits low to the ground (polished concrete floors), it is slightly elevated on a concrete plinth that frames the living space. "You can use the plinth for displaying objects or keep it quite simple," says Gong.

And although the fireplace provides a central focus to the open-plan living areas, an automatic blind can be released between the living and dining areas to create a more intimate space.

Sense of permanence

173

Inarc Architects

This substantial home was designed as a weekender for a couple with an extended family. The house has been designed in two wings. One wing includes the main bedroom, ensuite and sitting area/parents' retreat. The other wing has been designed for children and includes bathrooms, guest accommodation and a second living area. The main living areas, including the kitchen and dining areas, are in the middle of the two wings.

A massive fireplace in the living area forms the spine of the house. Made of Kyneton basalt, the fireplace extends across almost the entire living area. "It was the first thing that was built. It took two people eight months to build," says architect Reno Rizzo, co-director of Inarc Architects. The basalt is in hues of oranges and greys, depending on where it was excavated. "It's a dry stone wall construction. The entire wall was built without mortar. Each piece was chiselled by hand to ensure a perfect fit," says Rizzo.

The fireplace is set into the massive stone wall on a plinth, also made of basalt. To ensure the fireplace appeared recessed into the wall, the architects lined the fireplace with black steel. Black steel beams and columns were also used to divide the three functions of the fireplace; the central fireplace is flanked by an area for wood storage on one side and space for a television on the other. An arm attached to the television allows the screen to be tilted towards the lounge. "We wanted the fireplace to appear as one continuous slot in the wall," says Inarc co-director, Christopher Hansson.

The stone fireplace is particularly important in the overall design of the house, which is predominantly made of basalt, recycled iron bark, steel and glass. "Timber generally has a shorter lifespan and is considerably lighter than the stone. The two materials tend to balance each other," says Rizzo, who incorporated basalt in the exterior of the house.

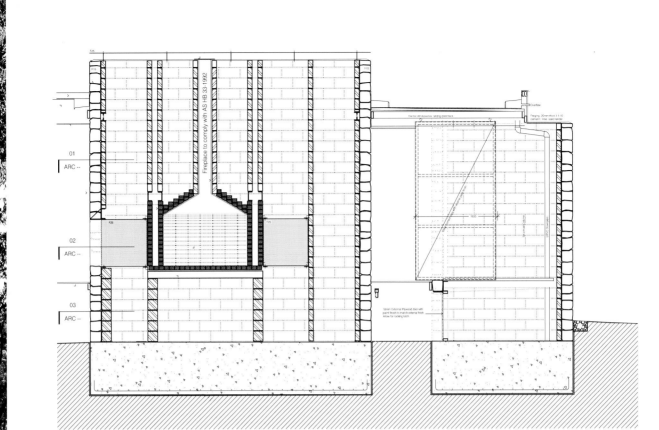

Simple arrangement

Architect Greg Gong

This fireplace is located in a new living wing that was added to a 1930s home. "Originally, there was no family room," says architect Greg Gong, who designed the extension for his own home. "The living and dining rooms were quite separate," he adds.

The contemporary addition leads directly onto a side garden, which is bathed in light for most of the year. However, with floor-to-ceiling glass and an absence of curtains, the room required additional heating (central heating is included in the design). "I love the idea of building up a wood fire," says Gong. "It's not just the glow of embers. It's also the light it creates. It's quite magical."

The fireplace, which is framed in steel, features a 20-millimetre-thick steel ledge that cantilevers 300 millimetres above the polished timber floorboards. "Originally the alcove (next to the fireplace) was designed for a television set. But it could also be used for storing wood," says Gong, who prefers to keep the living room space uncluttered.

As Gong and his wife have a large collection of books, they were also keen to include shelving in the design. The bookshelves have been 'slotted in' behind the fireplace, next to the frameless window to the courtyard. There is also a separate bookshelf lining the wall in the bedroom located above the fireplace. "The two bookshelves combined create a fairly strong acoustic control," says Gong.

While the fireplace is a focal point during the colder months of the year, the courtyard-style garden creates its own attraction. Planted with Japanese maples, there's a glow from the garden during autumn. "I've always seen the fireplace as an anchoring point. After that's been designed, the furniture can fall into place. And like the fireplace, I like to be surrounded by fairly simple furniture."

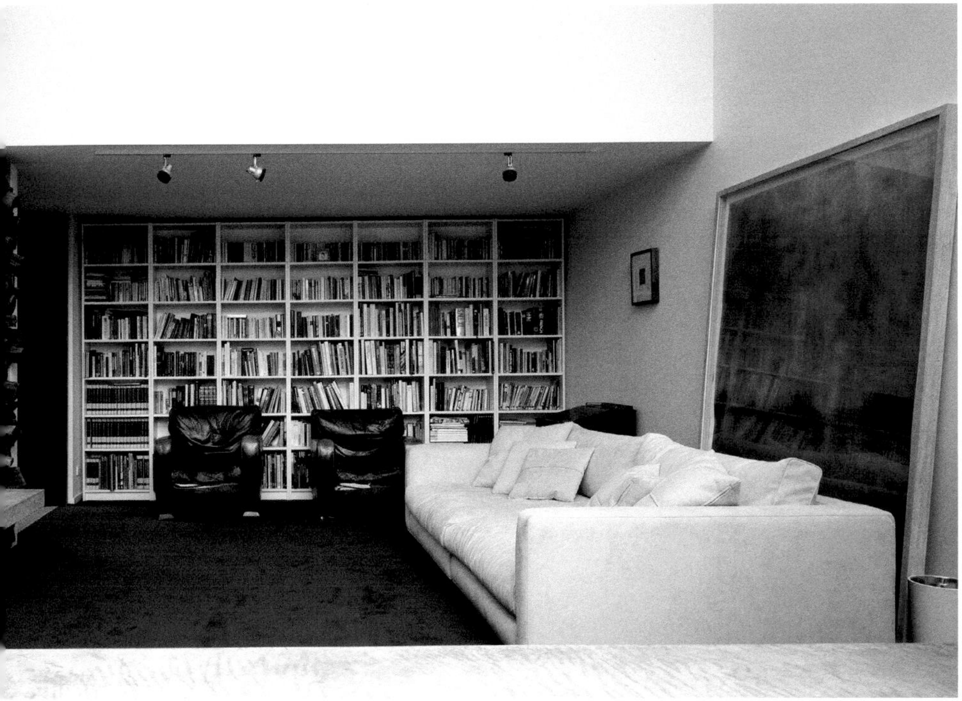

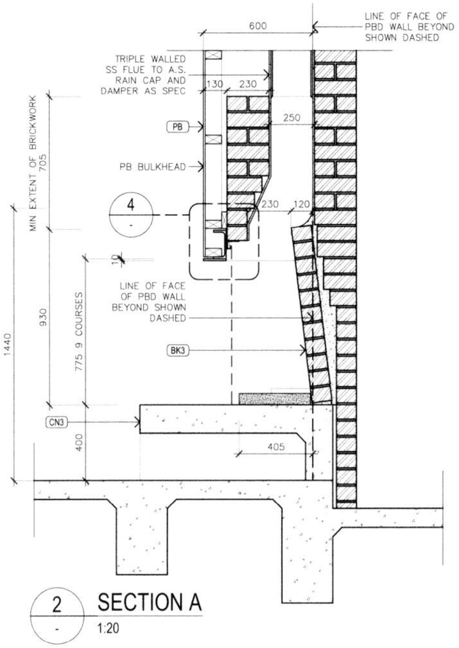
600
LINE OF FACE OF PBD WALL BEYOND SHOWN DASHED
TRIPLE WALLED SS FLUE TO A.S. RAIN CAP AND DAMPER AS SPEC
130
230
250
PB
PB BULKHEAD
MIN EXTENT OF BRICKWORK
705
4
230
120
10
LINE OF FACE OF PBD WALL BEYOND SHOWN DASHED
1440
930
775 9 COURSES
BK3
CN3
400
405
2
SECTION A
1:20

Warming faces

Coy & Yiontis Pty Ltd

Architects George Yiontis and Rosa Coy were keen to include a fireplace in their home. Located on the ground floor of their two-storey house, the fireplace can be found in the library that leads directly from the couple's main living area. The room is given several names by their three children: the library, parents' retreat and the tall room (after its 5-metre-high ceilings).

The library is lined with bookshelves and deep couches and armchairs. And while the focus of the room is towards the fireplace during cooler evenings, there is also a strong connection to the central courtyard. Large sliding doors open to create an almost verandah-like space. The 900-millimetre-wide concrete bench seat that frames two sides of the library can be used as an outdoor seat or internally to watch the glowing embers.

The fireplace sits on the concrete bench that doubles as a hearth. "We kept the side of the fireplace open, rather than closing it in. We wanted to make sure the heat spread to the entire room rather than just being channelled in one direction," says Yiontis, who was also keen to create a sense of 'floating' above the ground.

Set into the plaster walls, the fireplace is lined with refractory bricks. "These bricks have a high silica content. They store the heat. They're the same bricks they use in kilns," says Yiontis, who used the same bricks to create a two-tiered fire grate. "We wanted to be able to draw air up the chimney," he adds. The fireplace is elevated to head height, so the family can easily enjoy the heat. »

To avoid going outside to collect firewood, a 600-millimetre alcove adjacent to the fireplace is used to store wood. As Yiontis says, "We have hydronic heating in the house. But there's nothing like looking at an open fire, holding a glass of red wine".

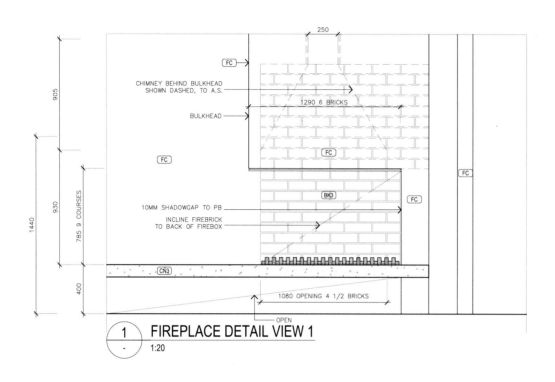

CHIMNEY BEHIND BULKHEAD
SHOWN DASHED, TO A.S.

1290 6 BRICKS

BULKHEAD

FC

FC

10MM SHADOWGAP TO PB

INCLINE FIREBRICK
TO BACK OF FIREBOX

BK3

FC

905

1440

930

785 9 COURSES

400

250

FC

CN3

1080 OPENING 4 1/2 BRICKS

OPEN

1 **FIREPLACE DETAIL VIEW 1**
- 1:20

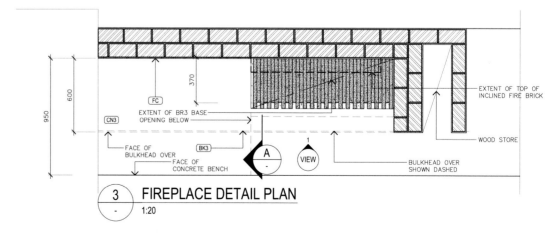

EXTENT OF TOP OF
INCLINED FIRE BRICK

370

FC

EXTENT OF BR3 BASE
OPENING BELOW

CN3

950

600

WOOD STORE

FACE OF
BULKHEAD OVER

FACE OF
CONCRETE BENCH

BK3

A
-

1
VIEW
-

BULKHEAD OVER
SHOWN DASHED

3 **FIREPLACE DETAIL PLAN**
- 1:20

SKYLIGHTS

Architects Ink

This four-storey Victorian terrace home in Paddington, Sydney, has been completely remodelled and extended by Architects Ink. Included in the renovation is a new kitchen that extends to a side street. "We wanted to bring additional light into the kitchen. And it wasn't possible to include windows," says architect Pierre Della-Putta.

The 6- by 2.5-metre skylight in the kitchen extends the entire length of the space. The architects angled the glass skylight/roof to ensure they met the local council's height restrictions and to create extra ceiling height in the galley-style kitchen.

To control the amount of light entering the kitchen, motorised aluminium louvres were integrated into the skylight. "The kitchen louvred glass roof permits controlled daylight, sunlight and heat penetration into the space," says Della-Putta, who was also keen to protect the beech veneer joinery from weathering. When the louvres are left open, sunlight can penetrate into the adjoining dining area.

A skylight was also included in the attic of the house. This skylight was also fitted with louvres. But while the louvres in the kitchen primarily control heat, those in the attic prevent artificial light from appearing above the rooftop at night. "The house falls within a heritage precinct (overlooking Sydney Harbour). Artificial light could detract from the heritage value of the Victorian home's slate roof," says Della-Putta.

188

189

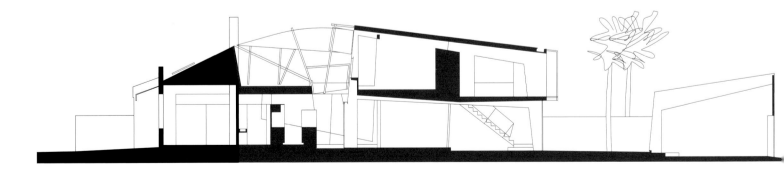

Michael Rahill Architect

This small Victorian terrace house was completely redesigned by architect Michael Rahill. The only remnants of the original house are the façade and verandah, together with the two party walls and one internal wall. The remainder of the house is completely new, with kitchen, bathroom, laundry, living and dining areas on the ground floor and two bedrooms and a bathroom on the first floor.

The new design is organised around two courtyards to increase natural light penetration into the house. The first courtyard allows north light into the living room and main bedroom and, by reflection from the two-storey north facing wall, into the kitchen.

Light provided by the courtyards is supplemented by skylights that allow direct sunlight into those rooms that don't face north. Together the courtyards and skylights create a light-filled house.

A small skylight appears in the passage towards the front of the house. It provides a shaft of sunlight that dramatically animates the space. A second skylight, 3 metres long, cuts through the ceiling of the bathroom and extends into the kitchen. Both skylights are located in an outdoor deck above the service spaces. The 200-millimetre-thick glass in the skylights is level with the timber decking and is designed to be walked on.

A third skylight at the rear of the house brings north light into the stairwell and into the dining area below. It also provides light to a small study nook in the second bedroom. Three spaces are served by one skylight. "I like the skylights to work hard," says Rahill.

Most new internal room divisions are made of cupboards or sliding panels. These divisions generally do not extend to the ceiling but stop short, with the gap to the ceiling closed with clear glass

highlights. By this means, light from the skylights permeates the surrounding spaces. These divisions are finished in dark richly glossy plywood panels that provide mysterious deeply contrasted reflections of light.

A skylight also brings natural light into the garage, located at the rear of the property. Made of polycarbonate, this skylight cuts a swathe from one end of the garage to the other, extending to form a slot window at the north end.

As Rahill says, "When you are hemmed in on all sides you must find the light from within the site or from above. Skylights have the ability to effectively defy the circumstances of the site".

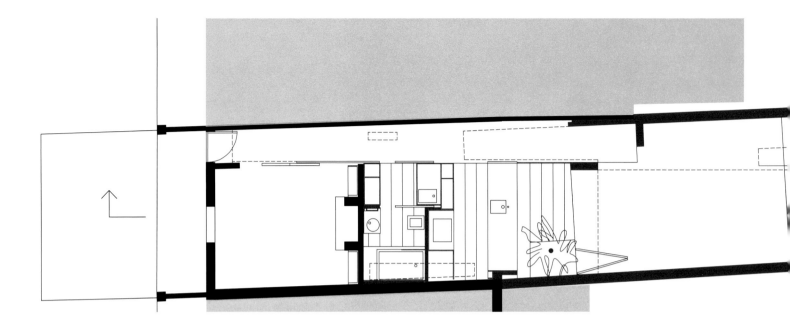

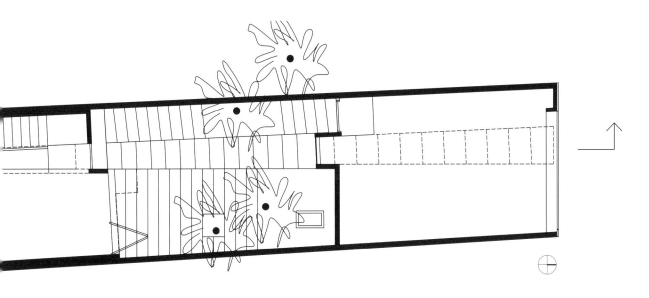

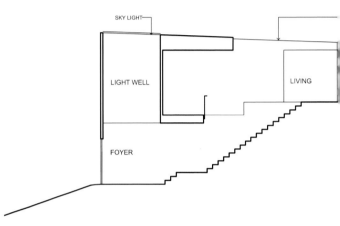

SKY LIGHT

LIGHT WELL   LIVING

FOYER

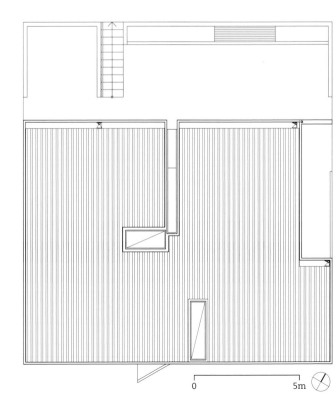

0   5m

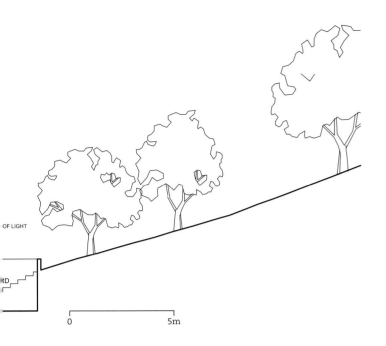

OF LIGHT

RD

0   5m

Terroir Architects

This house is surrounded by towering eucalypt trees, even though it is only 2 kilometres from the centre of Hobart, Tasmania. The two-storey house is nestled into the side of a hilltop. "The house is oriented to capture the views of the city," says architect Scott Balmforth of Terroir Architects.

While the vistas are impressive, the site, surrounded by bushland, suffered from a lack of natural light. To remedy this problem, the architects inserted a number of skylights into the Zincalume roof. Some of these skylights are rectangular in form, while others extend down walls.

One of the main skylights appears in the roof, above the central staircase. Approximately 3 metres long, it allows light to filter into the core of the house, lighting the entrance on the lower level. To increase the amount of light at ground level (which includes the garage), an additional skylight was inserted into the roof. However, unlike the skylight over the staircase, which connects with plaster walls, this one is clad in plywood and stained red. "We wanted to add some visual interest as well as creating a sense of arrival," says Balmforth. "There's a red glow that spills over the stairs," he adds.

Skylights were also integrated into the bathroom on the first floor. Located in the centre of the floor plan, the bathroom and separate toilet lacked natural light. The solution was to create a 900- by 1500-millimetre glass roof over the shower as well as including a highlight window in the adjacent toilet.

While Hobart doesn't suffer from days of excessive heat, the architects were conscious of reducing heat loss as well as heat gain. As Balmforth says, "You need to be concerned about the temperature. But it's also about using the natural light to enliven the spaces".

199

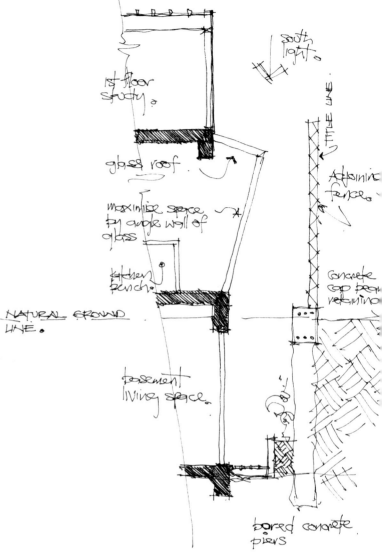

1st floor
study.

south
light.

glass roof.

maximise space
by angle wall of
glass.

kitchen
bench.

NATURAL GROUND
LINE.

basement
living space.

title line.

Adjoining
fence.

concrete
cap beam
retaining

bored concrete
piers

Col Bandy Architecture

The owners of this inner-city home wanted a relatively large house on their compact, 230-square-metre site. When architect Col Bandy was given the brief to design the new house, he realised he would have to create an extremely large hole in the ground to fulfil the owners' requirements. "There was simply not enough land to provide three bedrooms and separate living areas without going down," says Bandy, who created a 7- by 10-metre hole in the ground.

Two bedrooms, a bathroom and the wine cellar are at basement level, the kitchen and living areas are at ground level and the main bedroom, ensuite and study are on the top level. "The house was zoned to allow for independent living," says Bandy. "The lower level feels a bit like a London basement flat, but with more light," he adds.

One of the most critical aspects of the design was getting natural light into both the basement and the ground-floor kitchen and living areas. "We were quite restricted by the distance from the side boundary," says Bandy, who cleverly inserted a light well adjacent to the kitchen. Floor-to-ceiling glass windows framed in aluminium have been angled 7 degrees out to the garden, to capture the light. This bank of windows extends to form a skylight, allowing light to filter onto polished concrete floors.

A plinth-like garden in the light well allows sunlight to filter into the basement rooms. The top level, containing the main bedroom, has also been skewed 10 degrees in relation to the middle level, to allow additional light into the home. As Bandy says, "The skylight draws light into the darkest part of the house. But it was also conceived to allow light into a neighbouring property. We didn't want to create a blank three-storey wall for either the owners or neighbours to look at". And while the courtyard garden doesn't permit full planting, there's sufficient room and light for bamboo to grow.

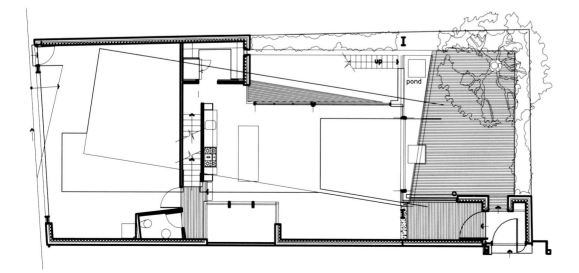

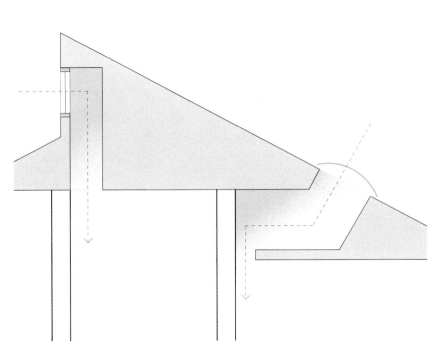

Robert Simeoni Architects

This house was built in the 1970s. While the three-level house (one level is used for basement car parking) was unusual in design, it presented a particularly unwelcoming entrance. "It was quite tight, as well as being fairly dark," says architect Robert Simeoni, who was keen to open up the entrance and to link the three levels within the home.

One of the devices used to open up the entrance was the insertion of a new front door. Unlike the original solid timber door, the new door is framed with frosted glass panels. The original curved timber staircase was removed and a simple, more streamlined staircase was inserted.

However, the greatest improvement to the entrance was the insertion of two skylights in the roof, directly above the staircase. These skylights, 1.2 metres long by 0.6 metres wide, were designed to allow a spill of light (and warmth) onto the wall rather than the full exposure of usual skylights. Fluorescent and halogen lighting concealed in the skylights creates a soft glow at night. Simeoni also included a third 'crevice' in the roofline, directly above the stairs. This alcove features only artificial lighting.

"We wanted to create subtle shafts of light rather than walking in and feeling overwhelmed by the light, whether during the day or at night," says Simeoni.

209

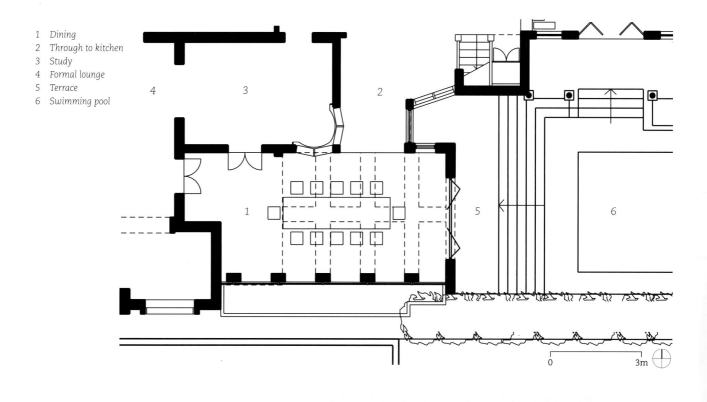

1 Dining
2 Through to kitchen
3 Study
4 Formal lounge
5 Terrace
6 Swimming pool

4

3

2

1

5

6

0   3m

Stephen Jolson Architect Pty Ltd

This 1920s Spanish Mission-style home suffered from having small windows and low ceilings. So when it came to a renovation, a light-filled and spacious dining area was part of the brief. "This dining area was previously an outdoor terrace. There was an opportunity to create a contemporary pavilion, one that brought in the natural light," says architect Stephen Jolson.

The new dining area, located near the kitchen, features massive timber beams, running vertically and horizontally across a glass cube. While they appear solid, the oak beams have been carefully crafted onto steel frames concealing glass joins in the process. "It would have been almost impossible to create continuous glass walls. And that approach would have been fairly pedestrian," says Jolson, who spaced the beams just over a metre apart.

The design for the glazed pavilion, with a glass roof, was initiated by a set of French timber doors, with an accompanying frame, bought by the owners of the house. "They wanted us to design a pavilion that would complement these period doors. Our solution was to create a contemporary design, using timber in a different manner," says Jolson, who also increased the ceiling height of the dining area to 3.5 metres (as opposed to 2.7 metres in the original home).

While the dining area, which leads to a pool and terrace, is filled with natural light during the day, at night artificial light comes from external sources. "We've used fairly strong lights outside, below floor level. The light is refracted from the walls," says Jolson. "For dinner parties, candles on the dining table set the mood," he adds.

Index of architects

213

Acknowledgments

I would like to thank all the architects featured in this book, along with the owners of these homes with such superb architectural details. Thanks must also go to the many photographers who contributed. Their images allow these wonderful details to be fully appreciated. I would also like to thank my partner Naomi for her support and literary criticism.

Stephen Crafti

216

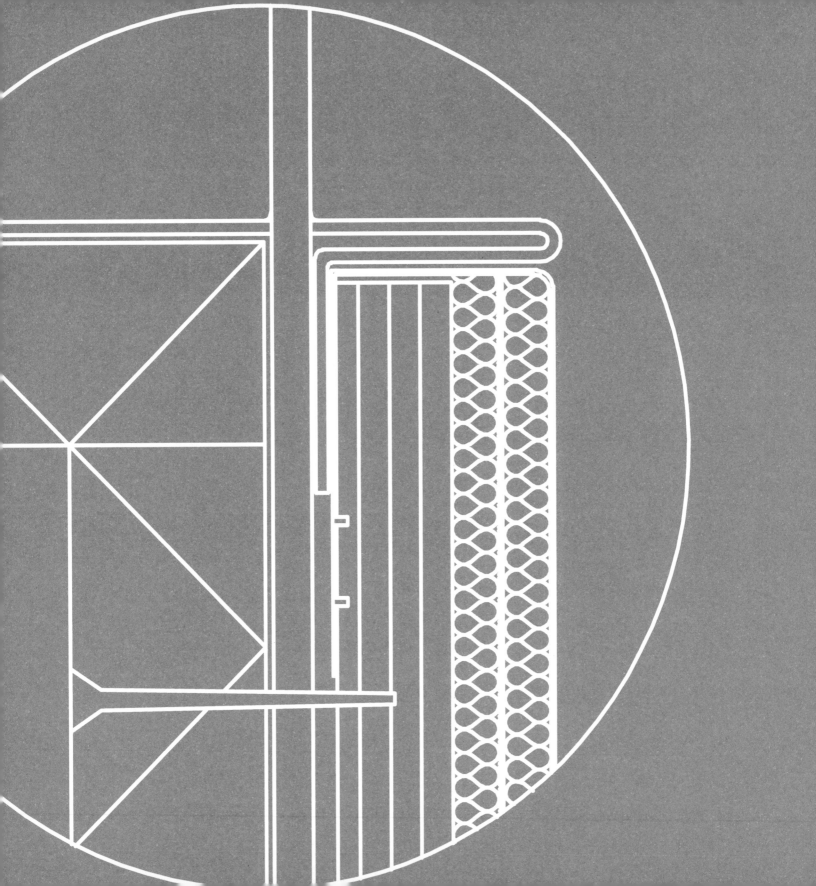